The Highlights Book of
HOW

Highlights

The Highlights Book of
HOW

DISCOVER THE SCIENCE BEHIND HOW THE WORLD WORKS

HIGHLIGHTS PRESS
HONESDALE, PENNSYLVANIA

Parents and Caregivers,

For your child's safety, we have carefully developed the activities in this book so they can be performed and enjoyed by children age seven years or older. The activities specify how difficult an activity is and when children should ask an adult for help.

However, since children develop at different levels, only a parent or close adult can judge the abilities of a particular child. Please review individual activities to ensure they are appropriate for your child.

The Editors

For information about permission to reprint selections from this book, please contact permissions@highlights.com.

Published by Highlights Press
815 Church Street
Honesdale, Pennsylvania 18431
ISBN: 978-1-64472-849-9
Library of Congress Control Number: 2022933270
Manufactured in Dongguan, Guangdong, China
Mfg. 07/2022

First edition
Visit our website at Highlights.com.
10 9 8 7 6 5 4 3 2 1

Editorial and Production: WonderLab Group, LLC
Design: Design Superette, Nicole Lazarus
Production: Margaret Mosomillo, Lauren Garofano, and Jessica Berger
Editors: Andrea Silen and Marlo Scrimizzi
Cover Illustration: Tom Jay

Acknowledgements

Many people contributed to making this book. Without their creativity, dedication, and expertise, this gigantic book would not have been possible. We'd like to thank all the contributors!

WRITERS: Libby Romero, Jennifer Szymanski, Paige Towler

ILLUSTRATORS: Scott Burroughs, Hayelin Choi, Todd Detwiler, Avram Dumitrescu, Tom Jay, Dan Sipple

PHOTO RESEARCH: Annette Kiesow

REVIEWERS: Thomas Alexander, Alden Denny, Emily Denny, Laura Figueroa, John Flanigan, Karen Girg, Adele Igel, Matthew Igel, Robert Roberts, Akiko Shinya, Lucy Spelman, David Weiss, Grant Wilson

OTHER CONTRIBUTORS: Connie Binder, Caitlin Conley, Lori Merritt, Maya Myers, Molly Reid

We'd also like to thank those who previously created the art and select activities for *Highlights* magazine that appear in the book.

CONTENTS

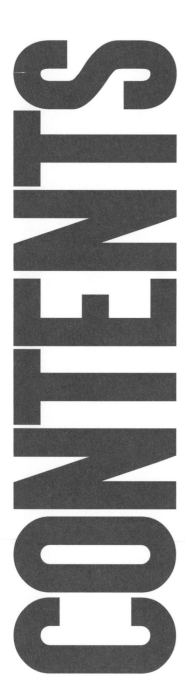

Human Beings

Amazing Animals

Digging Up Dinosaurs

The Great Outdoors

Wild Weather

The Ocean

Outer Space

Fantastic Food

Fun and Games

Making a Difference

INTRODUCTION

Dear Reader,

After creating an activity adventure in *The Highlights Book of Things to Do*, we here at Highlights found that there was still more out there to get curious about. Whether we were building a fort outdoors, creating an animal mask, or cooking up a gift for a friend, we found that almost every activity had some sort of cool science behind it. And we wanted to know more. So we asked ourselves lots of questions . . . most of them began with the word *how*. What we learned is that this word opens up a world of possibilities.

That's why we decided to create our new book, *The Highlights Book of How*. Throughout these pages, the simple question of "How?" will take you on an exciting journey where cool explanations and fun activities help you discover the science behind how the world works.

Want to find out how we know about dinosaurs? Curious to learn how snakes slither? Ever wonder how the moon formed? Just ask "How?" and you will be swept into the ancient past, spirited into the wild, and rocketed into outer space to find answers. Asking "How?" can help you learn about dinosaurs, modern-day animals, everyday technology, and human beings. It can help you explore weather, the ocean, outer space, and the great outdoors. You can even learn about food and fun and games.

In this book, we cover questions that fall under all of these topics and more. But the fun doesn't stop once a question is answered. Science experiments and activities allow you to dive deeper into all of these topics. We've also included a final chapter called "Making a Difference" where you'll learn things like how to build a community garden and how to design an ocean cleaning machine. Everything in this last chapter was included to show you how you can make the world a better place.

But the most fun part about this book? Asking "How?" can have a snowball effect. Once you get the answer to one question, you will undoubtedly want to ask more questions! Fortunately, there's a lot out there to explore. We hope you enjoy the adventure!

Your friends,
The Editors at Highlights

How to Use This Book

There are no rules on how to use this book. You can open it to any page you'd like—and come back to any other page that interests you. If you know you'd like to learn how microwaves heat food, you can open up to the chapter called "Everyday Technology." Or if extreme storms are more your thing, you can go to "Wild Weather." If you want to learn more about the foods you eat, you can go to "Fantastic Food." And if you only have 10 minutes to spare, you might like to try out "6 Quick Challenges" at the beginning of every chapter. But you don't have to know exactly what you want to learn or do because we've given you dozens of science explanations to read and more than 100 activities to try.

STUCK? DON'T GIVE UP!

We've included a variety of activities that are simple, sort-of-simple, and not-so-simple. (Each activity features a star rating that tells you its level of difficulty.) If you get stuck on a challenging activity, we encourage you to find a grown-up who can help you get unstuck. In fact, there are many activities in here that are perfect—and fun—to do with grown-ups.

When you do an activity, don't worry if you make a mistake. Mistakes are important. They reveal new discoveries—including how to do something different next time. For instance, when we first tried to make the "cloud" that "rains down" food coloring on page 177, we used shaving cream for the cloud. It was extra creamy shaving cream. That was a mistake. No matter how much colored liquid we added, it never rained. The cloud sucked up all of the colored water. We realized that we needed to use something a bit less absorbent. We thought and thought. What could we use instead? Then we looked in the refrigerator and saw a can of whipped cream. Voilà! Whipped cream looks just like shaving cream but it's not nearly as thick. So when we used that for the cloud, the colored water dripped right through and the experiment was a success. If we hadn't been unsuccessful with the shaving cream, we never would have searched for another solution—and found another use for whipped cream besides being a great topping for chocolate pudding!

USING RECYCLED AND ECO-FRIENDLY MATERIALS

You can do almost all of the activities in this book with materials that are already in your home. We encourage you to use recycled, scrap, or environmentally friendly products as much as possible in activities that ask for paper, cardboard, plastic bottles, plastic containers, food coloring, and similar items. For activities that require a balloon, deflate the balloon once done. See if you can reuse the balloon, or properly dispose of it. For anything that cannot be recycled, we challenge you to come up with clever ways to repurpose it into something else.

NOTE: We explored whether the activities that ask for plastic straws could be achieved with the same success using paper straws. When they can't, we recommend that you look into recycling plastic straws in your area before disposing of them. When you do the "Saltwater Rainbow" experiment on page 196, make sure to use a reusable clear plastic straw. If the straw isn't clear, you won't be able to see your rainbow. What's great about making and doing things yourself is that it challenges you to be resourceful, curious, and creative. These types of thinking are needed more than ever to address the environmental challenges of our time.

We hope that this book will inspire you to consider what goes into the things you make and use, and how those things may impact the planet. It may not seem like it, but one person (like you!) really can make a difference. How? Build a bee hotel (pages 314–315), make a herbarium (page 321), or repurpose old things into new stuff (pages 324–325). Read the last chapter, "Making a Difference," for even more fantastic ideas.

SAFETY FIRST!

Many activities ask you to work with things that are hot and/or sharp. It is important to learn how to safely use tools and equipment that can be dangerous to work with. We have noted when it is necessary to have a grown-up help you. We also tell you when a grown-up will need to use a tool or piece of equipment for you.

EVERYDAY
TECHNOLOGY

Take photos of places in your neighborhood. With an adult's help, find each place on an online map.

Quick Challenges

Cut the cord—no computer, video games, music, or TV—for one afternoon. At the end of the day, write about everything you did without using technology. How did it make you feel?

Try to name a type of technology that starts with each letter of the alphabet. How many letters did you use?

Go on a technology scavenger hunt: Find five things in and around your home that beep, five things that use batteries, and five things that help you connect with others.

Write a message. Hold it in front of a mirror. Challenge a friend to read what you wrote.

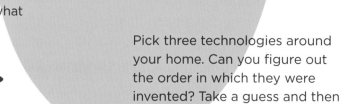

Pick three technologies around your home. Can you figure out the order in which they were invented? Take a guess and then research to find the answer.

How Do Microwaves Heat Food?

Microwave ovens may seem like they can warm up food without emitting any heat, but there is a lot going on that the eye can't see. When you press the START button on a microwave oven, a small tube within the machine, called a *magnetron*, begins to work. The magnetron creates a type of electromagnetic wave. *Electromagnetic waves* are waves of energy that have magnetic and electric fields. There are different kinds of electromagnetic waves, from the light you can see to the invisible waves used to communicate with someone on a cell phone.

In this case, the magnetron makes *microwaves*, very small waves of light we cannot see. These microwaves bounce around the inside of the microwave oven, where they come into contact with your food. Like all things in the world, your food is made up of teeny, tiny units called *molecules*. One example of a molecule is a a water molecule, which plays a very important role in the microwave oven: When the microwaves meet water molecules in your food, they make the water vibrate and bump into other molecules in the food. This movement creates heat! And with enough movement, there is enough heat for the food to get hot.

MICROWAVE PARTS

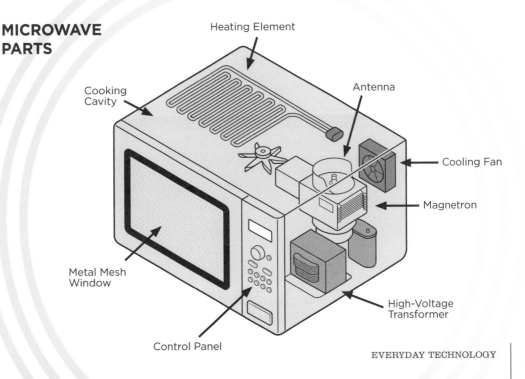

Heating Element

Cooking Cavity

Antenna

Cooling Fan

Magnetron

Metal Mesh Window

High-Voltage Transformer

Control Panel

MELTING AT THE SPEED OF LIGHT

With a microwave oven and a little bit of math, you can measure the speed of light in your kitchen!

You Need

- Microwave
- Chocolate bar
- Plate
- Oven mitts
- Ruler
- Paper and pencil or calculator

1. If your microwave oven has a turntable, remove it and any other spinning parts before you begin.

2. Place the chocolate bar in the middle of the plate. Heat it on high in the microwave for 15–20 seconds, or until the chocolate starts to melt.

3. Wearing oven mitts, carefully remove the plate from the microwave. It will be hot!

4. Look for melted spots in the chocolate. In centimeters, measure the distance between the center of two melted spots. This is half the wavelength of a microwave. Divide the measurement by 100 to convert it into meters.

5. Multiply your answer by two to get the full measurement of the wavelength in meters.

6. Find the frequency of the microwaves that your appliance uses to cook food. It's often written on a sticker inside or on the back of your microwave oven. If you can't find it, use 2450 MHz, which is standard for most microwaves.

Safety Tip

Ask for a grown-up's help with anything hot.

7. A frequency of 2450 MHz equals 2,450,000,000 waves per second. Multiply the full wavelength in meters (from step 5) by your microwave's frequency in waves per second. The answer should be close to 300,000,000 meters per second, which is the speed of light!

How It Works:
In this experiment, you can see a specific pattern of melting on the chocolate bar. This pattern shows the wavelength of the tiny waves of invisible electromagnetic light (microwaves) that power your oven. ∎

Did You Know

One MHz, or *megahertz*, is a measuring unit equal to one million hertz. Hertz was the name of a famous physicist who proved that electromagnetic waves (like the ones in your microwave oven) exist.

More Ideas

If you don't have a chocolate bar on hand, try this experiment with American cheese. Or scatter mini marshmallows or chocolate chips on a plate and measure the distance between two of them.

How Do Mirrors Reflect Images?

WHEN YOU LOOK INTO A mirror, you are looking at your own image reflected back at you. This happens in part thanks to the mirror's smooth surface. But we can't forget the thing that lets people see in the first place: light.

When a ray of light hits something you're looking at, such as a tree or your shoes, a part of the light bounces off the object. This reflected light then enters your eyes. There, it meets a special kind of cell, one of the tiny units that makes up your body. These cells are called *photoreceptors*. When light meets photoreceptors, they send signals to your brain. This allows your brain to interpret what you are seeing.

The same thing happens when light bounces off a mirror but with an important difference: Unlike most objects, mirrors are very, very smooth. Most mirrors today are made of a piece of glass covered with a thin, smooth piece of metal on the back. Other items—like polished stones or the surface of water—have been used as mirrors throughout history. Because materials like these are so smooth, when light hits them, almost all of it is reflected instead of just some. The light that hits the mirror bounces back and goes into your eyes, showing you a reflected version of yourself.

BUILD A FUN HOUSE MIRROR

You can make some really wild and wacky reflections when you build your own curved mirror.

★☆☆
Easy

Tip

Objects will look fuzzier if you use aluminum foil instead of mirror paper. For the best view, make sure to use the shiny side of the foil and make the foil as smooth as possible.

You Need

- Mirror paper (found at hobby stores) or new, unwrinkled aluminum foil
- Scissors
- Rectangular piece of thick cardboard
- Tape
- Small, colorful objects

1. Cut a piece of mirror paper or aluminum foil large enough to cover the cardboard.

2. Tape the paper or foil to the cardboard. The mirrored side should face up.

3. Hold the mirror upright with one long side on the table. Place a small object in front of the mirror. What does it look like?

4. Bend the mirror's sides away from you so its middle curves forward. Then pull the mirror's sides forward so its middle curves back. How does the image change when you change the shape of the mirror?

5. Repeat with other objects. Which wacky reflection do you like best?

How It Works:

When you look at an object, light reflects off it and bounces into your eyes. Your brain interprets that information. It creates a picture of the object for you to see. But your brain assumes that light travels in straight lines. When you look into a curved mirror, light bounces at odd angles. This fools your brain and causes you to see a distorted image.

MAKE A COLORFUL KALEIDOSCOPE

For more reflective fun, see what beautiful patterns you can create when you make your own kaleidoscope.

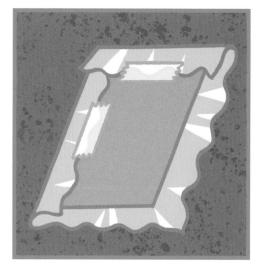

2. As smoothly as possible, wrap aluminum foil around the rectangle, shiny side out. Secure it with tape.

1. Draw a rectangle on the cereal box that is three inches wide and one inch shorter than your paper towel tube. Cut it out.

Tip

To make a shorter kaleidoscope, use an empty toilet paper tube instead.

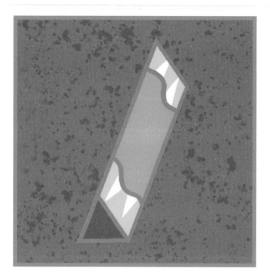

3. Fold the rectangle lengthwise into thirds to form a triangular tube.

4. Slide the triangular tube into the paper towel tube. Secure it with tape.

5. Use the permanent marker to trace around one end of the paper towel tube on the construction paper. Cut out the circle. Use a sharp pencil to poke a small hole in the middle of the circle. Tape the circle over one end of the tube.

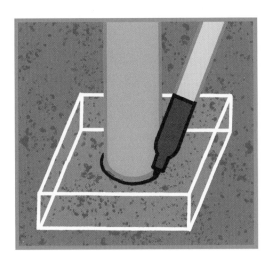

6. Trace around the end of the tube on the empty plastic container. Do this twice. Cut out both circles. Use scissors to trim them so they fit just inside the paper towel tube.

7. Push one plastic circle into the open end of the tube so it is flat against the end of the triangular tube. You may need to glue the edges to hold it in place.

8. Put the beads, sequins, glitter, and/or confetti on top of this plastic circle. Tape the other plastic circle to the open end of the tube.

9. Use wrapping paper or other supplies to decorate the outside of the tube.

10. Hold the finished kaleidoscope up to the light and look through the small hole. Turn it. Shake it. What do you see?

How It Works:
Light reflects off the shiny aluminum walls of the triangular tube in the kaleidoscope. It bounces back and forth between the walls and colorful objects inside. This creates beautiful color patterns that constantly change as you turn the kaleidoscope. ■

How Do Rockets Fly?

ROCKETS THAT CAN BLAST INTO space may be a recent invention, but rockets have been around for more than 800 years. The first known rockets were invented in China. According to legend, Chinese alchemists accidentally invented the fuel for these ancient rockets—gunpowder—while they were trying to create a potion for immortality. When the gunpowder was placed into a bamboo tube and set on fire, the explosion caused a big burst of hot gas to come out of the tube. When the gas was released, the tube shot away from the ground, creating a rocket.

If you've ever let go of an open balloon, you've seen how this works firsthand. When you fill a balloon with air or helium, the gas creates pressure that builds up inside the balloon. If you hold or tie the neck of the balloon closed, all that pressure is stuck inside. But if you let go without sealing the balloon—*whoosh!* The pressure causes the gas to force its way out of the balloon through the neck.

ROCKET PARTS

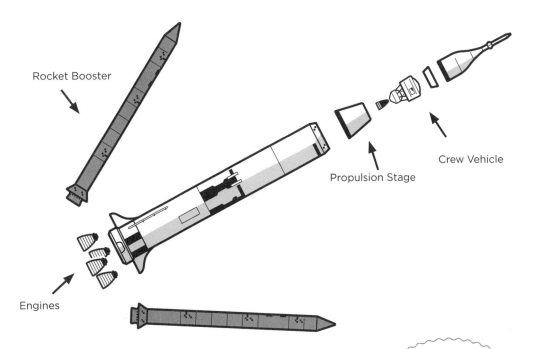

Rocket Booster

Crew Vehicle

Propulsion Stage

Engines

Now, all the force is exiting the balloon. This force pushes on the balloon, making it fly forward. The force that drives the balloon is called *thrust*.

Today, rockets still use thrust to push off the ground. But to get enough thrust to escape Earth's gravity and fly into space, rockets need a lot more power. Like early rockets, modern rockets use types of fuel to create huge amounts of hot gas that launch the rocket. A rocket's fuel is called *propellant*. To lift off, the rocket burns tons of propellant. As the fuel burns, it creates a lot of thrust, and the rocket shoots forward and blasts up toward outer space.

BALLOON-POWERED ROCKETS

Three . . . two . . . one! Blast off with this fun experiment that explores how forces make rockets work.

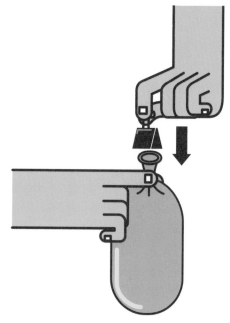

1. Before you begin, choose your flight path. For instance, it can be from the floor to the ceiling or from one doorknob to another.

2. Tie the fishing line or string to the starting point. If necessary, secure it with tape.

3. Pull the other end of the string through a straw.

4. Tie or attach this end of the string to the end of your flight path. The string must be tight so the "rocket" will move smoothly along its path.

5. Blow up a balloon. Pinch it shut with your fingers or hold it closed with a small paper clip. Don't let the air escape!

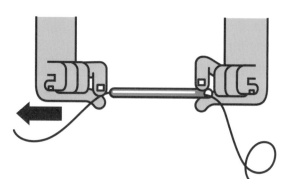

More Ideas

Build a rocket that travels from wall to wall (horizontally) and another one that moves from floor to ceiling (vertically). What's different about the two setups? Do the rockets fly the same?

6. Tape the balloon to the straw, continuing to hold its opening shut. Make sure the opening of the balloon is facing the starting point.

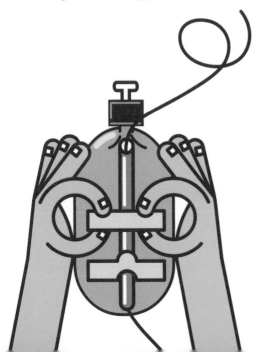

7. Ready, set, go! Let go of your balloon and see how far your rocket travels.

8. Remove the balloon from the straw and blow it up again. Hold the bottom of the balloon shut as you tape it back to the straw. Then attach a small paper cup facing upward on each side of the balloon. Put paper clips in the cups. Launch your balloon again and again. How many paper clips can your rocket carry? How far will it travel? ■

How Does Glue Hold Things Together?

GLUE AND OTHER ITEMS USED for sticking things together are called *adhesives*. People have been using natural adhesives for thousands of years. Some early versions of glue came from naturally sticky materials like certain plants and saps, while others were made by boiling animal skins.

Today, glue is usually a thick liquid or gel that can be spread easily and evenly over a surface. Most glue is made from artificial materials. These are usually man-made ingredients consisting of "sticky" molecules—tiny building blocks of matter—that like to stick to each other and to other surfaces.

These ingredients tend to be too sticky to use by themselves. So they are dissolved in something called a *solvent*. This makes the glue easy to spread. When you take glue out of its container and spread it over something, it seeps into tiny openings in the object. Once the glue is out of its bottle and exposed to the air, the solvent slowly evaporates—or becomes a gas instead of a liquid. Once the solvent is gone, the glue hardens and turns into a solid. Imagine putting glue on a piece of paper and pressing another piece onto it as the glue hardens. The molecules are sticking to themselves but also to the two objects. It's a sticky situation—but that's a good thing.

ARTWORK THAT STICKS

Glue holds things together. It can also help you make some cool crafts like suncatchers!

You Need

- Flexible plastic lid
- White glue (lots of it!)
- Food coloring
- Toothpicks
- Hole punch
- String

1. Fill the entire lid with a thick layer of glue.

2. Add a few drops of food coloring. Use different colors.

3. Swirl the food coloring around the glue with a toothpick. Don't swirl too much or your colors may look muddy.

4. Let the glue dry for two to three days.

5. Once the glue is fully dry, peel the suncatcher off the lid. Punch a hole in the suncatcher, tie a string through the hole, and hang your suncatcher in a sunny place. ■

More Ideas

Make window clings. Tape a sheet of plastic wrap to a table. Mix glue, a few drops of food coloring, and a few drops of liquid dish soap in a bowl. Place some cookie cutters on the plastic wrap and pour a thick layer of your mixture into each. Let dry and then remove the cookie cutters. Peel your designs off the plastic wrap and stick them to a window. Watch the sun shine through!

How Do Batteries Power Devices?

FROM HANDHELD VIDEO GAMES to instruments in a doctor's office to cars zipping around outside, batteries power electric devices everywhere. To give these things power, batteries store energy from chemicals, and then turn that energy into electricity. Most batteries are made up of three main parts: the electrolyte, the cathode, and the anode. The cathode and the anode are separated by the electrolyte, which prevents them from touching or interacting.

The electrolyte is made of a special mix of chemicals. When you turn on a battery-powered device like your television remote, the chemicals in the electrolyte start to interact and cause chemical reactions.

Did You Know

Some batteries are rechargeable. In these batteries, the same process happens as in a non-rechargeable battery. But then, thanks to a charger, the reactions happening in the battery can be reversed! This restores the charge to the battery.

PARTS OF A BATTERY

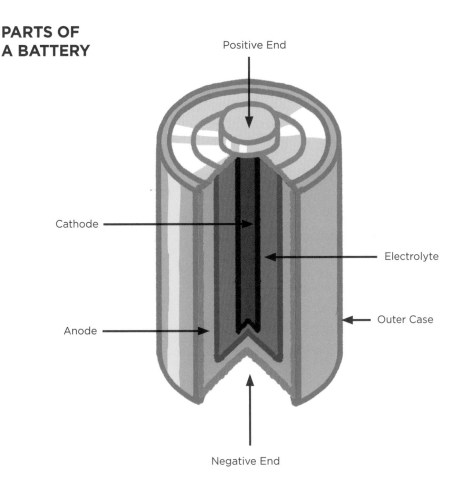

Positive End

Cathode

Electrolyte

Outer Case

Anode

Negative End

These chemical reactions cause lots of tiny, negatively charged particles called *electrons* to appear in the anode. Because objects with opposite charges attract one another, the negatively charged electrons in the anode are drawn to the positively charged cathode.

However, because of the electrolyte mixture in the way, the electrons are stuck and cannot travel through the battery. Instead, the electrons must

exit out of the anode and travel to the cathode along a wire in the device you are using. But the electrons don't all rush out at once. How fast the electrons move along the wire depends on the device and how much power it uses. While they are traveling, the electrons are the electricity that your device can use to do its job. The battery will keep making electrons while it is in a device until it runs out of electrolyte—in which case, it's time for a new battery.

MAKE A LEMON BATTERY

The job of a battery is to convert chemical energy into electrical energy. Lemons—with help from other materials—can do that!

1. Roll each lemon under your palm back and forth across a table. This releases the juice inside the lemons.

2. Make two small cuts on the top of a lemon, at least an inch apart. Have an adult help with anything sharp.

3. Insert a nail or washer into one cut and a penny or piece of copper wire into the other. Make sure they're inserted deep enough to touch the juice inside, but they should not be touching each other.

More Ideas

What happens when you use fewer lemons? What happens to the pennies and nails as time goes on? Try using other fruit instead of lemons, such as grapefruits or oranges. Do they work as well? Do vegetables, such as potatoes or carrots, work as well?

Safety Tip

Ask for a grown-up's help when using the sharp knife.

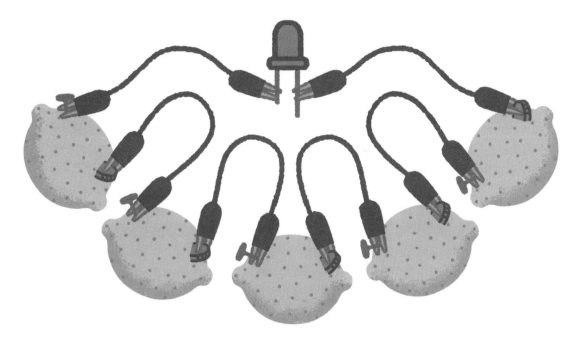

4. Repeat steps 2 and 3 with all of the lemons.

5. Line up the lemons. Make sure all of the pennies are on the right side and all of the nails are on the left side.

6. Using one of the electrical wires, connect the nail in the last lemon on your right to the penny in the second-to-right lemon. Repeat this with the second-to-right lemon and the one to its left. Keep going, using four wires.

7. Attach a clip of one of the last two wires to the penny on the far right lemon. Then connect the same wire's other clip to the longer leg of the LED diode. Attach the last wire to the nail on the far-left lemon and connect its other clip to the shorter leg of the diode.

8. The diode should light up! If it doesn't, make sure the pennies and nails are pushed into the lemons enough. You can also try wiggling them. Your circuit is complete.

How It Works:
In this experiment, the nail acts as the negative terminal, or the anode, of a battery. It releases electrons. The copper penny or wire acts as the positive terminal, the cathode. The cathode collects the electrons released from the anode. The positive and negative flow of electrons through the lemon juice changes chemical energy into electrical energy. When the terminals at each end of the lemons are connected to the opposite ends of the LED diode, the flowing electricity lights it up. ■

How Do Bridges Hold Weight?

BRIDGES LET PEOPLE AND CARS move across water and deep canyons. Some bridges have hundreds of thousands of people traveling over them every day. This means that bridges need to be able to hold incredible amounts of weight. Bridges around the world are designed to do the heavy lifting in different ways. But no matter the shape, size, or length of a bridge, it needs to balance two different forces that are caused by gravity and weight: compression and tension.

Compression is a force that pushes or squeezes inward. *Tension* is a force that stretches or pulls outward. The best way for a bridge to stay strong is to balance these forces, spread them out evenly, or transfer them to other areas so the bridge does not break.

Almost all bridges use at least two different parts to do this: abutments and piers. *Abutments* are the supports that sit at the ends of a bridge. These help direct weight

and pressure to the ground on either side of the bridge instead of to the bridge itself. *Piers* are the supports in the middle of a bridge. These channel pressure directly down into the ground. One of the most basic types of bridge, called a beam bridge, relies only on a straight beam supported by abutments or piers. But because these bridges tend to weaken the longer they get, engineers have had to design other ways of dealing with compression and tension.

Besides beam bridges, some of the oldest bridges are arch bridges. These use the shape of an arch to transfer weight and force it out to the abutments on either side. Over time, architects developed new types of bridges by adding frames with vertical and diagonal bars of strong materials to beam or arch bridges to help support them and distribute force. Bridges with these frames are called truss bridges. Cantilever bridges are made of small sections supported by trusses. But some of the most modern bridges, like cable or cable-stayed bridges, use strong cables to transfer force outward to piers and abutments.

PARTS OF AN ARCH BRIDGE

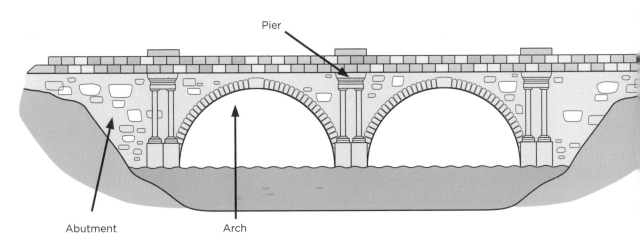

Pier

Abutment

Arch

BUILD A BRIDGE

Use paper and pennies to investigate how design impacts the strength of a bridge.

You Need

- **2 thick books that are about the same thickness**
- Ruler
- Plain white paper
- Pennies
- Tape
- Construction paper
- Cardstock

1. Lay the books about 10 inches apart on a table.

2. Place a piece of plain white paper across the books, like a bridge.

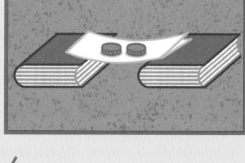

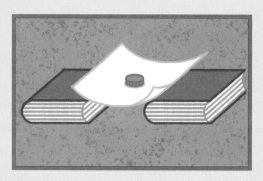

3. Place a penny in the middle of the paper. Add another one next to it. How many pennies can the bridge hold until it collapses?

4. Fold the paper in half lengthwise. Place the folded paper across the books. Repeat step 3. Does your bridge hold more pennies?

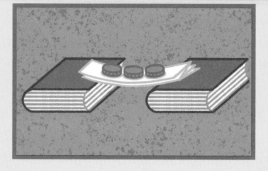

5. Fold the paper in half lengthwise again. Is this narrower, thicker flat bridge strong enough to hold a full row of pennies?

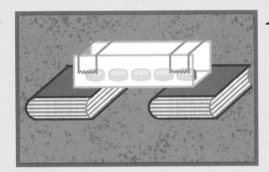

More Ideas

Find photos of really long bridges. Collect an assortment of supplies, such as different kinds of paper, wooden craft sticks, or straws. Use the supplies to create a long bridge that is strong and sturdy. Test your bridge with pennies.

6. Fold your paper lengthwise into thirds to create a U-shaped bridge with sides. Tape the top edges so the bridge doesn't unfold. Add a row of pennies. Did adding sides make your bridge stronger?

8. Fold the paper in different ways to change the shape of your bridge. For example, make it a two-lane bridge or change the height of the sides. Test to see how many pennies your bridge can support.

9. Test your ideas using different materials, such as construction paper and cardstock.

10. Which design and material resulted in the strongest bridge? ∎

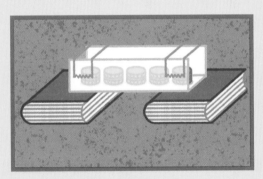

7. Stack another row of pennies on top of the first one. Can your bridge support a full row of stacked pennies? (If your bridge collapsed in step 6, set up the bridge again first. You can add a second layer of paper to make it stronger. Then add your rows of pennies, one layer at a time.)

How Does an Umbrella Open?

PEOPLE HAVE LONG WANTED TO stay dry when it rains—umbrellas have been around for some 4,000 years. The first umbrellas, or *parasols*, were probably used to keep out the sun, but soon, waterproof umbrellas appeared as well. These early umbrellas were made from oiled or waxed paper with stiff wooden handles. A version of the foldable umbrella was invented in France in the 18th century, but these more easily carried umbrellas didn't become common until the 20th century.

Today, umbrellas are made of waterproof fabric. This material is stretched over a frame of flexible spokes known as *ribs*. Each rib is attached to a thin piece of metal, called a *stretcher*, which attaches at the other end to a runner. The *runner* is a simple ring of material able to slide up and down the central shaft. When the runner is near the bottom of the shaft, the stretchers pull the ribs closed.

To open your umbrella, you push up on the runner, which in turn causes the stretchers to push outward against the ribs. This opens the top of the umbrella. Your umbrella then stays open thanks to a handy spring in the shaft that extends a small locking piece once the runner is all the way up. To close your umbrella, you press in the locking piece, and the process begins in reverse. Of course, you may want to dry it off first!

DESIGN AN UMBRELLA

Challenge yourself to build a better umbrella.

You Need

- Building materials, such as paper, wooden craft sticks, baking cups, coffee filters, paper plates, paper straws, etc.
- Scissors
- Glue
- Tape
- String
- Paper
- Pencil
- Small plastic cup
- Large plastic tub
- Cotton balls
- Small toy watering can
- Water

1. Examine all of your building materials. Brainstorm ideas about how to use those items to make the best umbrella.

2. Draw a sketch of your idea.

3. Use the materials to build the umbrella you designed in your sketch.

4. Put the plastic cup upside down in the plastic tub. Put a cotton ball on top of the cup. Then place your umbrella over the cotton ball.

5. Fill the watering can with water. Slowly sprinkle the water over your umbrella. Did the cotton ball stay dry? If not, brainstorm a new idea for a better umbrella and then build and test it. ∎

Tip

There is no one right way to do this experiment. Just think about what an umbrella needs to do. Then pick the materials that you think will do that job the best.

How Do Light Bulbs Light Up?

A LIGHT BULB MAY SEEM TO MAKE light out of nothing, but what you are seeing is actually a transformation. Light bulbs light up by turning light energy into electrical energy. For most of human history, humans used flame-based lamps to light up the dark. But in the 1700s, people began to understand more about electricity. In the early 1800s, scientists and inventors were able to harness electricity to create early versions of light bulbs. Later, others—including the famous inventor Thomas Edison—improved on the invention to create the first versions of the incandescent light bulb we still use today.

Although the incandescent light bulb is an amazing feat of science, it consists of very simple parts: a glass shell, a metal base, and thin wires. When a light bulb is connected to an electrical source, the electricity runs through its wires. Two of these wires are there to conduct the electricity and provide support to the third and most important wire: the filament. The *filament* is a thin, coiled piece of metal called tungsten. Tungsten is difficult for electricity to travel though. Because of this, when the

electricity reaches the tungsten, it has to use a lot of energy to keep traveling. This energy causes the tungsten atoms to vibrate, which generates heat. When the tungsten gets hot enough, it will begin to glow, converting the heat to light.

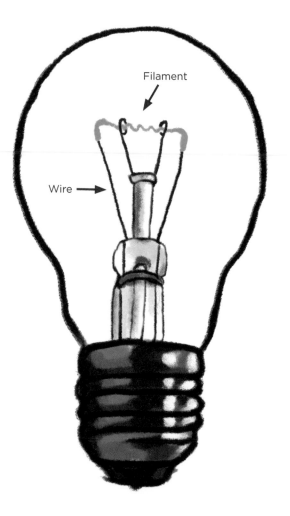

Filament

Wire

Hot tungsten can set things on fire. It is also in danger of rusting if it comes into contact with the oxygen in our air. This is where the glass shell comes in. When the glass shell is made in a factory, all the air is removed from inside, creating a vacuum. This keeps air away from the tungsten filament. Talk about a bright idea!

Did You Know ?

Though we can't see the vacuum inside a light bulb, if you accidentally break one, you might hear a loud pop. That noise is the sound of air rushing in!

BRILLIANT BULBS

Today, we use a few different types of light bulbs. Check out this history of light bulbs:

• **1930s:** The fluorescent light is developed as an alternative to the incandescent light bulb. You might see these lights when you go into a store, a classroom, or another large room. Fluorescent lights can be made in different shapes, like tubes. Inside the glass, fluorescents have a type of gas and a few mercury atoms floating around. The inside of the glass is also coated with white phosphor powder. When electricity passes through the gas as it travels from one end of the bulb or tube to the other, the energy causes the mercury atoms to emit *ultraviolet light*. This is an invisible wavelength of light we cannot see—that is, until it hits the phosphor. It's actually the phosphor reacting to the ultraviolet light that gives off the white, very uniform light we do see from fluorescent light bulbs.

• **1960s:** Inventors create a type of bulb called the LED. That stands for *light emitting diode*. Like incandescent bulbs, LEDs change electric energy into light. However, they don't use heat. Instead, these lights direct electricity through a special type of material called a *semiconductor*. When the electric current passes through, the semiconductor emits light. This process is called *electroluminescence*, and it is much more efficient than the way an incandescent light bulb makes light.

• **1990s:** Engineers take the LED a step further, creating the organic LED, or OLED. OLEDs use an organic material for their semiconductor. OLEDs are energy-efficient like LEDs. But they are usually manufactured in thin sheets, which companies use to make very thin screens for products like TVs, smartphones, and handheld gaming consoles.

SET UP A CIRCUIT

Learn how to create a circuit by making either a mini cardboard tent to light up the night or a silly face with a light-up nose.

You Need

- Piece of cardboard (for tent) or a short cardboard tube (for face)
- Scissors
- LED diode (3 or 5 millimeters; found in hardware and hobby stores)
- Masking tape
- Aluminum foil
- Clear tape
- 2 AA batteries
- Rubber bands
- Markers

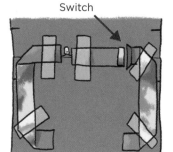
Switch

4. Fold, cut, and tape down the strips and diode using clear tape, as shown.

5. Tape the batteries together so one positive end meets a negative end.

LIGHT-UP TENT

1. Fold the cardboard in half. Cut four notches—one on either side of the fold on both long sides.

2. Bend apart the legs of the LED diode, and place it in the center of the cardboard.

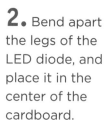

3. Press three long strips of masking tape onto aluminum foil. Then cut them out.

Foil

Tape

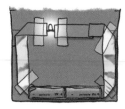

6. Tape the ends of the batteries to the foil side of the strips. Place a rubber band around to hold them in place.

7. Fold the cardboard, wrapping a rubber band around the notches. Decorate the tent.

8. Press down on the switch (shown at top) to light the diode. If it doesn't light up, flip the direction of the diode's legs.

LIGHT-UP FACE

1. Cut the cardboard tube in half lengthwise. Poke a hole through the center of one half.

2. Bend apart the legs of the LED diode and place it on top of the half-tube without a hole.

3. Press three long strips of masking tape onto aluminum foil. Then cut them out.

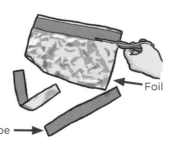

Foil

Tape ➞

Switch ➞

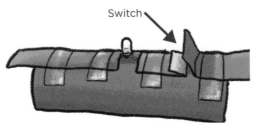

4. Fold, cut, and tape down the strips and diode using clear tape, as shown.

5. Tape the batteries together so one positive end meets a negative end.

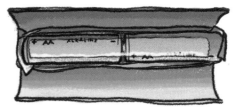

6. Tape the ends of the batteries to the foil side of the strips. Place a rubber band around them to hold them in place.

7. Press down on the switch (shown at the bottom left) to light the diode. If it doesn't light up, flip the direction of the diode's legs.

8. Put the two half-tubes together. Push the lit diode through the hole in the other tube. Draw your silly face!

How It Works:
The LED diode lights up when an electric current passes through it, like one from a battery. The electricity moves in a circle, from the battery to the diode and back, through metal connectors called conductors. This circle of electricity is called a *circuit*. ■

HUMAN
BEINGS

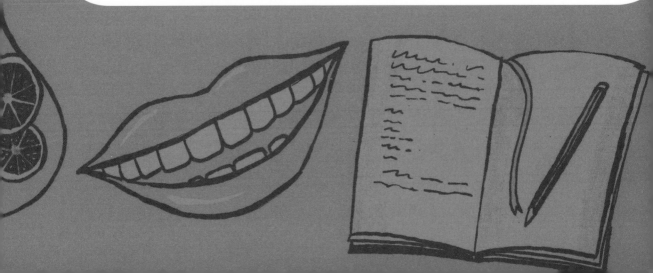

Put small objects, such as pencil erasers, wadded up pieces of paper, or small, smooth rocks, on the floor. Try to pick them up with your toes and put them in a cup.

Quick Challenges

Try to do different activities—like brushing your teeth, combing your hair, and holding utensils—with your nondominant hand. What does this feel like? Does it get easier with practice?

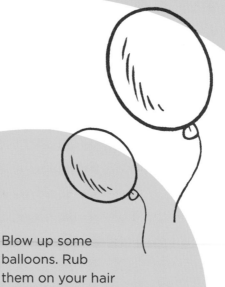

Blow up some balloons. Rub them on your hair and try to get them to stick to a wall.

Go outside, close your eyes, and breathe deeply. Identify everything you can smell.

Search your home for things that feel soft, hard, smooth, and rough. What other textures can you find?

Take a poll of your family and friends. How many of them can roll their tongues or wiggle their ears?

How Does Hair Grow?

WE HAVE HAIR SPROUTING FROM our heads to our toes—even inside our ears and nostrils. Regardless of where it is or how long it grows, all human hair is made from the same stuff.

Hair is made of a protein—a type of molecule—called *keratin*. This is the same substance that makes up your fingernails—it's also the same material found in a horse's hooves and a rhinoceros's horns! The part of the hair that you see growing out of your skin, called the *shaft*, is not alive. This is why it doesn't hurt when you cut your hair. But beneath the skin, something else is happening.

Your skin is full of tiny, tubelike organs called *follicles*. Inside each follicle is a group of cells that make keratin. This is known as the *root* of the hair. The root is connected to lots of small blood vessels, which help bring nutrients to create the keratin. As more and more keratin grows, it pushes up and out of the follicle. Eventually, it grows into the hair you can see—including the hairs inside your nose!

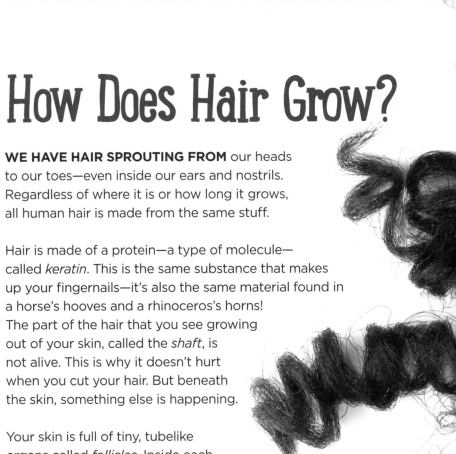

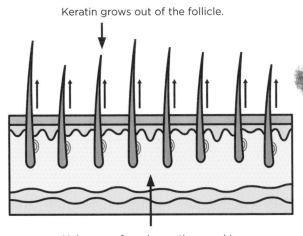

Keratin grows out of the follicle.

Hair grows from beneath your skin.

MAKE YOUR OWN SHAMPOO

Does all that keratin on your head need a good wash? You can make your own shampoo at home!

You Need

- 1 cup water
- 1 cup unscented castile soap
- 1 teaspoon light vegetable oil or glycerin
- 1 teaspoon essential oil, such as lavender or lemon
- Empty shampoo bottle

1. Combine all ingredients in the shampoo bottle.

2. Swirl the bottle to mix the ingredients.

3. The shampoo is now ready to use!

Safety Tip

Before doing this activity, make sure that you're not allergic to any of the ingredients.

HAIR STRENGTH INVESTIGATION

Put your hair to the test to see just how strong it is.

Medium

Tip
Don't pull hair out of your head for this experiment. You can find plenty of hair on your comb or brush.

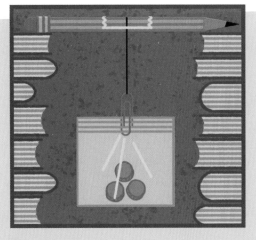

You Need

- 1 or more strands of hair (at least 5 cm long)
- Pencil
- Tape
- Small paper clip
- Small plastic bag
- 2 equally tall stacks of books
- Pennies
- Kitchen or postal scale

1. Tie or tape one end of a strand of hair around the middle of the pencil and the other end to the paper clip.

2. Hook the paper clip through the top of the plastic bag.

3. Gently pull on the pencil and the bag. Reattach the hair more securely if it comes loose.

4. Stack the books into two equal piles on a table. Lay the pencil across the top of the books. If the bottom of the bag touches the table, add more books so the piles are higher.

5. Guess how many pennies you can put in the bag before the hair breaks. How much do you think the pennies will weigh?

6. Now test your hypothesis. Add pennies, one at a time, to the bag.

7. When the hair breaks, weigh the bag on the scale. Count the pennies in the bag. Compare the results to your prediction.

How It Works: A single hair is very thin, but it's made up of three different layers. The inner layer is soft and fragile. The middle layer contains rodlike bundles of keratin. The cells in the outer layer overlap— like fish scales. Together, these three layers create an incredibly strong strand of hair. ∎

How Do
We Sneeze?

IT STARTS AS A TICKLE IN YOUR nose, then—*achoo!* You've sneezed. What causes sneezes, and how do they happen?

Sneezing is one way for your body to protect itself. Your nose is very important. It is one of the main ways you take in air. Because of this, your body has lots of ways of keeping out foreign objects like dust, pollen, or other things that could irritate you. Some of these protections include nose hairs and, yes, mucus. But if those things don't work, your body might turn to sneezing out whatever is bothering it.

Your nose is lined with many cells, nerves, hairs, and irritant receptors. These body parts are all responsible for doing different jobs or sending different messages to your brain. Some cells interpret and analyze scents. Nerves respond to feeling and touch. And the hair and irritant receptors respond to certain chemicals. But sometimes, when these body parts encounter an irritant such as dirt or pollen, something else happens. The parts of your inner nose send a message to alert a special part of your brain that something is in your nose that's not supposed to be. This part of the brain controls sneezing.

To cause a sneeze and get rid of whatever is irritating your nose, your brain sends messages to make muscles move in certain parts of your body. Your eyes close, and your tongue usually moves to the top of your mouth. Your brain tells muscles in your chest and throat and around your lungs to start squeezing. These squeezes put pressure on your lungs, driving air suddenly and forcefully out of your nose. *Gesundheit!*

If you have to sneeze and don't have a tissue, sneeze into your elbow! And if you're sick, make sure to stay away from others. These steps can help reduce the spread of germs.

SNEEZING STYLES

People's bodies generally trigger sneezes in the same way, but that doesn't mean that all sneezes are the same. Check out some things that can cause unique sneezes.

Photic Sneezes

Photic sneezing is the term for sneezes that are caused by bright light. For some people, stepping out into the sunshine or looking at bright lights can trigger the sneeze reaction. Scientists aren't yet sure why this happens.

Multiple Sneezes

If you sneeze more than once in a row, that may be because your body wasn't able to get rid of the irritant on the first try.

Loud Sneezes

Are you an extra-loud sneezer? That probably means that your lungs have room for lots of air or you breathe in deeply before sneezing. The more air expelled at once, the louder the sneeze tends to be.

ACHOO CHALLENGE

How far do you think a sneeze travels?
Try this experiment to find out.

You Need

- Newspaper or parchment paper
- Tape
- Measuring tape
- Pencil
- Small bowl of water
- Food coloring
- Small saucepan
- 3 tablespoons gelatin, such as Knox
- Fork
- ¼ cup corn syrup
- Dropper or small spray bottle
- Tissues
- Turkey baster

1. Before you begin, go outside and create your testing area. Lay out a line of newspaper or parchment paper. Tape the sides to the ground.

2. Measure and mark every foot, up to 20 feet.

3. Create "thin snot." Pour water into a small bowl. Stir in a bright color of food coloring.

4. Create "thick snot." With an adult's help, heat half a cup of water in a small saucepan. Remove the water from the heat when it starts to boil. Add the gelatin and a different bright color of food coloring. Stir with a fork to break up the clumps as they begin to form. Add the corn syrup. Stir very slowly with the fork as the thick snot cools. Add a table-spoon of water if it gets too thick.

5. Once your thick snot is completely cool, you're ready to begin testing. Fill the dropper or small spray bottle with thin snot. Stand at the end of your testing area. Hold the dropper or spray bottle nose-high and squeeze. Examine the sneeze pattern you

Tip

Using bright colors of food coloring will make it easier for you to see and measure your results.

Safety
Tip

Ask for a
grown-up's help
with anything
hot.

create. Measure and record the distance the droplets traveled and the width of the sneeze pattern.

6. Repeat step 5 five times. Wipe the paper as clean as possible between each attempt. If the paper gets too wet, lay out another strip of newspaper or parchment paper to create a new testing area.

7. Repeat, using the same utensil (dropper or small spray bottle), with the thick snot. Remember to record your results.

8. Test in different ways. Hold the dropper or bottle higher or lower when you "sneeze." Use less snot in your dropper or bottle. Squeeze harder or softer. Use a turkey baster to make a bigger sneeze. Hold a tissue in front of the dropper or bottle when you release the snot.

9. Examine the results. Calculate the average distance the droplets traveled for each type of sneeze. (Add up the five distances and divide by five.) Calculate the average width for each type of sneeze. (Add up the five widths and divide by five.)

How It Works:
Viscosity is the measure of a fluid's resistance to flow. Thick liquids have a higher viscosity than thinner liquids. They are more resistant to flow. In this experiment, that's why the thin snot travels farther and wider than the thick snot. ∎

How Do We Fall Asleep?

SOME NIGHTS, YOU MIGHT FALL asleep right away. Others, you might toss and turn, waiting for your body to do its magic. What is it that causes humans to fall asleep, and why?

Scientists believe that sleep gives your body time to heal and refresh itself. This is also a time when your brain is extra busy. During sleep, your brain processes information and helps store memories. Your brain is also responsible for causing you to sleep in the first place.

When it is time for you to sleep, your brain releases a sleep hormone. For many mammals, this happens when you are low on energy, or when it is dark out. The hormone makes you feel drowsy. Meanwhile, your brain tells your muscles to relax and makes your breathing slow and steady. As your brain regulates all your body functions, you slip into unconsciousness. Now your brain can get to work on its important jobs, while you drift through dreamland.

KEEP A DREAM JOURNAL

Dreams can inspire your imagination or help you look at problems in a new way. To help you remember your dreams and understand what they might mean, keep track of them in a dream journal.

You Need

- Notebook
- Pencil or pen

1. Choose a small notebook for your dream journal and keep it by your bedside. Decorate it if you want. No one else has to read it unless you want them to.

2. Most dreams slip away when you get out of bed, so grab your journal as soon as you wake up and write down whatever you can recall. You might remember only a small part of it or what you felt like in the dream.

3. You don't have to use only words. You can draw pictures to show what you remember or how you felt.

4. Write the date of your dream and give it a title, such as "I Can Fly" or "The Chase." You can also label the type of dream it was: funny, crazy, adventurous, scary, etc.

5. As you fill the notebook, go back and flip through your old dreams. You might find similar plots or themes. Enjoy all the creative ideas your brain came up with. ■

WHY DO DREAMS HAPPEN?

Dreams are pictures, thoughts, or feelings that happen when you sleep. Experts have lots of ideas about why dreams happen, but no one really knows the exact reasons. Dreams may be a way for you to build memories or work through emotions. They may help your brain organize thoughts or analyze something you did that day. Or dreams may just happen—for no reason at all.

How Do Ice-Cream Headaches Happen?

WHEN YOU HAVE A BEAUTIFUL bowl of ice cream sitting before you, it can be tempting to wolf it down as fast as possible. But watch out—doing so could lead to an ice-cream headache. Also known as brain freeze, these headaches can occur when people eat or drink something cold very quickly.

Scientists aren't totally sure why ice-cream headaches happen. However, they think it might have to do with the blood vessels near the back of your mouth. When you slurp up a chilly food or drink, it passes across the roof of your mouth and the back of your throat. In these areas, you have lots of small blood vessels. *Blood vessels* are the veins, arteries, and capillaries that carry blood around your body.

Scientists think that when something very chilly touches these blood vessels, the cold causes them to squeeze suddenly. Then, once the cold item slides down your throat, the vessels warm up and quickly relax. Some scientists think that this can cause discomfort because the process sends a lot of blood to your brain at once. Others think that the unpleasant feeling might also come from the vessels squeezing and relaxing so quickly, which your brain interprets as pain.

The good news is that ice-cream headaches are not dangerous, and they go away very quickly. You can try speeding their exit along by pressing your tongue or thumb against the roof of your mouth or drinking warm water.

CHILLY CHOMPERS

On top of brain freeze, eating or drinking something too cold can cause a strange, somewhat unpleasant feeling in the teeth for lots of people. This is because inside the tough exteriors of your teeth is fleshy tissue called *pulp*. And inside this pulp are a lot of nerve endings, which send messages to your brain to let you feel things. When you bite into something too cold—or hot—the nerve endings in your pulp might send an alert to your brain, causing that strange feeling.

Did You Know?

Although it is sometimes called an ice-cream headache or even brain freeze, this sensation has an official medical term: sphenopalatine ganglioneuralgia.

HOMEMADE ICE CREAM

With a lot of tossing and just a few simple ingredients, you and a friend can make your own ice cream.

FOR TWO SCIENTISTS

You Need

- 1 cup whole milk
- ¼ cup sugar
- ½ teaspoon vanilla
- 1 quart-size zipper freezer bag
- 1 gallon-size zipper freezer bag
- 20 cups ice
- 1½ cups rock salt (available in some supermarkets)
- Winter gloves (optional)

1. Put the milk, sugar, and vanilla in the quart-size freezer bag. Squeeze out the air, then zip the bag completely closed. (If it is not sealed tightly, you will end up with salty milk.)

2. Place the small bag in the large bag.

3. Pack ice almost to the top of the large bag.

4. Ask an adult to pour one cup of the rock salt on top of the ice. Zip the large bag completely closed.

5. Toss the heavy bag back and forth for five minutes. It's best to do this outside in case anything drops or opens. You may also want to wear gloves because your hands will get cold.

6. Inside, open the large bag and drain out any excess water. Don't pour it on grass or other plants—salt water will kill them.

7. Have an adult add the rest of the rock salt and as much ice as will fit. Seal the bag again, then toss it back and forth for five more minutes outside.

8. Check the small bag. Do you have ice cream yet? You probably do, but if it's still runny, seal everything back up and toss it around for a few more minutes.

9. Scoop your ice cream into a bowl and add your favorite toppings: strawberries, sprinkles, whipped cream, or whatever you want. Dig in!

How It Works:
The rock salt lowers the freezing temperature in the bag—turning ice into super cold water. The cold water flows around the bag of milk as it is being tossed, cooling it down. When the temperature of the milk reaches its freezing point, it becomes ice cream. The more the ice cream is tossed, the smaller the ice crystals will be, making the ice cream creamier. ■

How Do Baby Teeth Fall Out?

DURING THE FIRST SEVERAL years of their lives, kids do a lot of growing. Not only do they grow taller, but their bodies, including their jaws, also grow larger. However, your teeth can't grow like the rest of you does. So the smaller teeth you started with need to be replaced with bigger, stronger teeth—and with more of them!

Your teeth are made up of a tough material called dentin. They are protected by a hard coating known as *enamel*. Inside each tooth is a tissue called *pulp*. This pulp is home to nerve endings and blood vessels. The pulp ends in a root that secures the tooth into your jawbone.

When it is time for a kid to lose their baby teeth and grow larger adult teeth—often around the age of six—special cells start to dissolve the root of each tooth. Once most of the root is gone, the tooth falls out! After that, adult teeth that have been growing beneath the gums start to move up into the empty spaces.

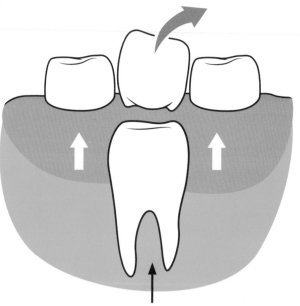

After a baby tooth's root dissolves, it falls out.

A new, adult tooth grows up from the gums to replace it.

MAKE "TOOTH PLAQUE"

Whether you have baby teeth or adult teeth, you have to watch out for plaque! *Plaque* is a film of bacteria that can cover your teeth. Do this experiment to model how sugar makes the bacteria grow. Then read on to find out how you can stop plaque in its tracks!

You Need

- 2 16-ounce clear cups
- 2 cups warm water
- 2 packets dry yeast
- 1 tablespoon sugar
- 2 spoons

1. Add one cup of warm water to each cup.

2. Add one packet of yeast to each cup.

3. Add one tablespoon of sugar to one of the cups.

4. Stir the cups with different spoons.

5. Watch the cups. In which one did the yeast grow?

How It Works:

Yeast is a fungus that gets energy from sugar. In this experiment, you can see how that energy causes the yeast to grow. The same thing happens with the bacteria in your mouth. The bacteria, called plaque, feeds on sugar. It breaks the sugar down into an acid that destroys the enamel on your teeth. This creates cavities, or holes in your teeth. To get rid of plaque, brush your teeth twice a day and floss regularly. ∎

How Do We Taste Food?

MMM, DO YOU HAVE A FAVORITE food? Most of us do, thanks to the tiny sensory organs on our tongues that let us taste things.

Everyone's tongue is covered in tiny bumps, called *papillae*. The papillae are home to small organs known as *taste buds*. Taste buds are what allow you to sense the flavor of a food. When your taste buds touch your meal, tiny hairs on the taste buds send signals to your brain to process the taste.

But it's not just your tongue—your nose and your spit also work to help you taste. When you smell a scent, it can send a message to your brain about the flavor. Your saliva helps things along by keeping your tongue moist and breaking down the food, which is necessary for your taste buds to work.

Scientists think that humans developed our ability to taste to help us survive. Being able to taste means that we're able to recognize nutrient-rich food and stay away from bad-tasting foods that might make us sick.

So far, scientists have labeled five basic tastes: sweet, salty, sour, bitter, and savory. Some scientists think that even more things should be considered tastes, including spiciness, mint, and fat.

FAVORITE FOODS

Do you love some foods more than others? That's totally natural! But why is it that foods you find appealing might seem gross to other people?

Some food preferences are inherited from your parents and other relatives; others are influenced by the foods you've grown up eating. And still others—such as loving salty and sweet foods—have to do with our ancient ancestors. Sugar and salt are important for human survival. But neither would have been very easy for humans to get long ago. Cravings for salt and sugar made humans look for foods that contained these ingredients, which helped them stay healthy back when the ingredients were scarce.

COLORFUL TASTE TEST

You taste with your mouth. But do your eyes influence taste, too? Let's find out!

You Need

- 5 pitchers
- Water
- Lemonade
- Food coloring
- Spoon
- Table
- Several volunteers
- Saltine crackers
- 3-ounce paper cups
- Paper
- Pen or pencil

1. Fill one pitcher with water.

2. Make another pitcher full of lemonade. Divide that lemonade equally into four pitchers.

3. Add red food coloring to one pitcher of lemonade, blue to a second pitcher, and green to a third

pitcher. Stir the food coloring in with a spoon. Your lemonade should be brightly colored. If it isn't, add more food coloring.

4. Do not add any food coloring to the fourth pitcher of lemonade.

5. Set up a table outside. Set your pitchers in a row: water, red lemonade, blue lemonade, green lemonade, and plain lemonade.

6. When your first volunteer comes by, tell them you are testing to see which kind of lemonade tastes best and ask if they would like to help.

7. If so, have the volunteer drink a glass of water and eat a saltine cracker. This will clear any existing tastes from their mouth.

8. Pour a small amount of lemonade from each pitcher in separate cups. Have the volunteer taste from each cup, drinking water and eating a cracker in between. Ask the volunteer to rank the cups of lemonade from sweetest to most sour. Record the results.

9. Now, have the volunteer close their eyes. Hand them the cups of lemonade in random order. Without them looking, have them taste from each cup, drinking water and eating a cracker in between each one. Ask the volunteer to rank the cups of lemonade again. Record the results.

10. After testing the lemonade, examine the results. Did your volunteer rank the lemonade in the same order both times? Or did the colors impact their perception of sweet and sour lemonade?

How It Works:

Some volunteers might notice that all the lemonade tastes the same. If so, congratulate them on their superior taste buds! Other people may prefer one cup of lemonade over the rest. Their sense of taste is influenced by how they associate the colors they see in the cups with other sweet and sour foods. ■

Tip

Don't reveal to your volunteer that all the pitchers of lemonade are the same until you complete testing. You don't want to influence their opinions.

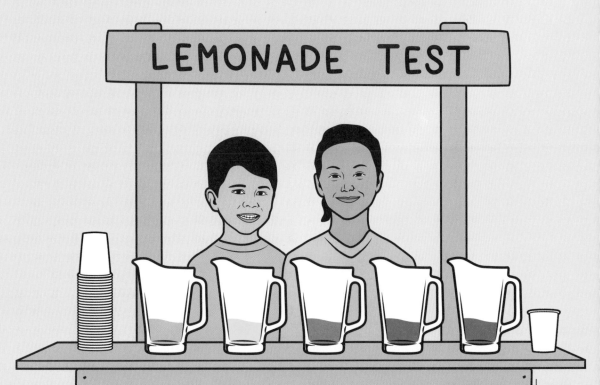

LEMONADE TEST

How Do We Hiccup?

YOUR BODY IS A SUPER well-functioning machine—most of the time. But it can make mistakes. Hiccups are small "oops!" moments caused by your diaphragm.

Your *diaphragm* is a muscle that sits below your lungs. Normally, it works to help pull air into your lungs. When your diaphragm squeezes, it pulls down on your lungs, helping them expand and fill with air. Then, when it relaxes, it pushes the air back out. But if your diaphragm becomes irritated, it can start to *spasm*, or quickly squeeze and relax.

These spasms can happen when you eat or drink too quickly, when you eat something spicy, when you accidentally swallow air, or even when you are feeling nervous or excited. As your diaphragm squeezes, you inhale a quick burst of air. Once the air hits your voice box—the part of your body that creates sound for you to speak—it causes a squeaky noise!

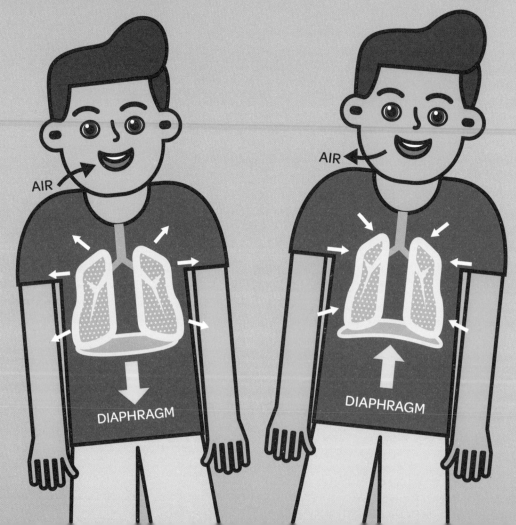

AIR

DIAPHRAGM

AIR

DIAPHRAGM

HICCUP NO MORE

Hiccups normally don't last very long, and almost always go away on their own. But they sure can be annoying! While there is no one tried-and-true cure for hiccups, there are several methods that don't work for everyone but could work for you. Here are some remedies you can try.

- Drink a glass of cold water
- Breathe slowly into a paper bag—but stop if you get dizzy
- Try to distract yourself with an activity, such as a game or show
- Hold your breath and count to 10

Did You Know?

It isn't just humans! Most mammals—from dogs to cats to squirrels to horses—have been known to get the hiccups.

BUILD A MODEL DIAPHRAGM

Breathe in. Breathe out. Now construct a model that shows how a muscle called the diaphragm helps you breathe.

You Need

- Clear 16-ounce plastic cup
- 2 small balloons
- 1 large balloon
- Scissors
- Tape
- 2 straight straws

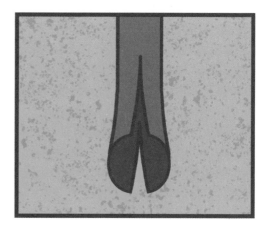

FOR TWO SCIENTISTS

1. Cut a hole in the middle of the cup's bottom. The hole represents your mouth and nose. The cup is your chest cavity.

2. Cut the necks off the two smaller balloons. These balloons are your lungs.

3. Cut one straw into two equal pieces. Each piece should be half the height of your cup. These short straws are your bronchi.

4. Tape each of the smaller balloons to the end of a short straw. Make sure no air can escape.

5. Cut the other straw so it is the same height as your cup. Make a two-inch cut in one end of this straw, splitting the end in half. This straw is your trachea.

6. Slide a small straw onto each split end of the longer straw, forming a Y. Tape the junction so it is sealed tightly.

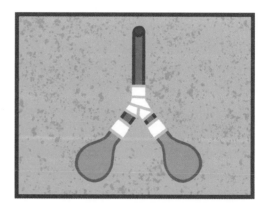

7. Hold the cup upside down. As you do so, push the longer straw through the small hole. The balloons should be completely inside the cup.

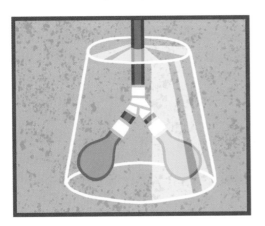

8. Cut the end of the straw that is poking through the small hole so it is split into four equal pieces. Fold the pieces down and tape them to the the cup.

9. Stretch out the large balloon. Tie at its neck. Cut off its top.

10. Stretch the tied part of this balloon over the large opening of the cup. This balloon is your diaphragm. Your model is now complete.

11. Gently pull down the diaphragm. What happens to the lungs? Let go of the balloon. What happens to the lungs now?

How It Works:

When you breathe in, air travels into your nose and mouth. It moves down your *trachea*, or windpipe, into two main bronchial tubes that lead into the lungs. The air then travels into smaller bronchioles and finally into tiny air sacs called *alveoli*. As you breathe in, your diaphragm, the muscle below your lungs, is pulled down. This creates more space in your chest cavity so the sacs (and as a result your lungs) can fill up with air. When you exhale, the diaphragm is released. There is now less space, and air is pushed back out of your lungs. ■

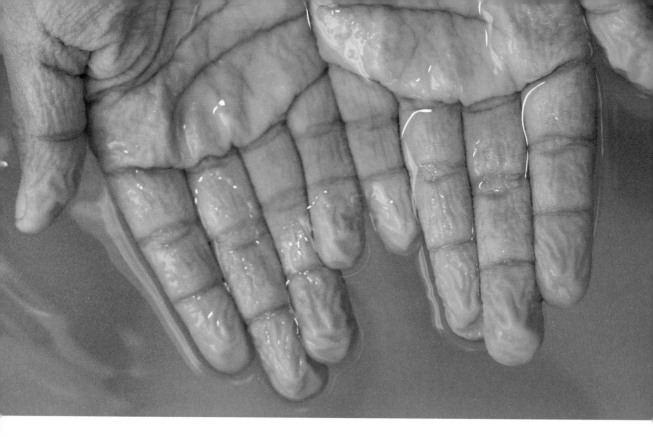

How Do Fingers Become Wrinkly in Water?

IF YOU'VE EVER HAD A NICE SOAK in a bath or gone for a long swim, you know that your fingers—and toes—tend to get wrinkly from the water. Is this just a random reaction? Nope, your body has a reason for doing this.

For a long time, scientists thought that water entering the outer layers of thick, dead skin in our hands and feet caused the skin to expand, making it wrinkle and puff up. Recently though, scientists have discovered that your body wrinkles in the water on purpose. When you

are in the water for a while, your body sends a message that causes the blood vessels in your hands and feet to squeeze tight. This also squeezes in the skin, making it wrinkle.

But why would certain parts of your body need to wrinkle? Wrinkled fingers and toes make it easier for humans to grip things when they are in the water. It can help us hold objects or avoid slipping on wet surfaces. So the next time you see your skin start to "prune," give your body a thank-you!

WRINKLY SKIN CHALLENGE

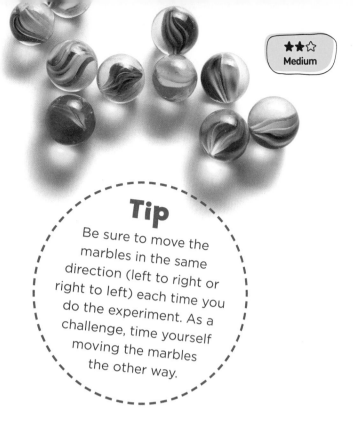

★★☆
Medium

Try this fun challenge to see if wrinkly fingers can help you pick up wet objects.

FOR TWO SCIENTISTS

You Need

- 2 small bowls
- 10 marbles or other smooth, round objects, such as glass beads
- Warm water
- Stopwatch
- Large bowl

Tip

Be sure to move the marbles in the same direction (left to right or right to left) each time you do the experiment. As a challenge, time yourself moving the marbles the other way.

1. Place two small bowls next to each other. Put 10 marbles or beads in one of the bowls.

2. As quickly as possible, pick up the marbles or beads one at a time with one hand, pass them to the other hand, and put them in the other bowl. Have a friend keep time with a stopwatch. Record the results.

3. Pour water into the bowl with marbles or beads. Race to see how quickly your dry hands can transfer the wet objects. Record the results.

4. Now, fill the large bowl with warm water. Hold both hands in the water for five minutes, or until your fingertips are all wrinkly. While you do this, have your friend dry off the marbles or beads and bowls.

5. Repeat the experiment with wrinkly fingers and wet and dry marbles or beads. Record the results.

6. Switch roles and have your friend move marbles or beads while you keep time. Under which conditions did you each move the objects the quickest? Are your results the same? ∎

Did You Know

Scientists think the creases in people's fingers may have developed over time. Having creases made it easier for our ancestors to pick up food in wet places.

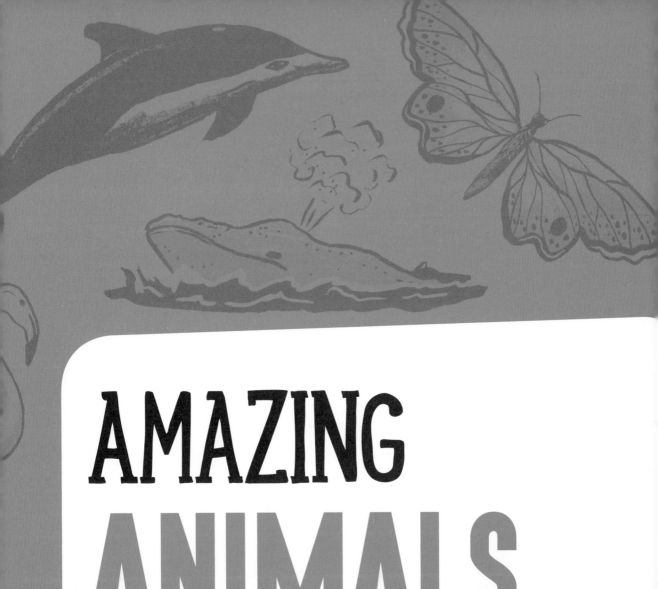

AMAZING
ANIMALS

Quick Challenges

Play animal charades with a friend. Act out an animal and have your friend guess which animal it is.

Come up with a code using animal sounds. For example, an *oink* can mean, "Hi!" A *moo* can mean, "How was your day?" Have a conversation with a friend using your animal sound code!

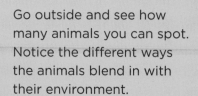

Go outside and see how many animals you can spot. Notice the different ways the animals blend in with their environment.

Think of your favorite animals. Do they have feathers, fins, fur, or something else? Look up how these features help them survive.

Challenge a friend or family member to name as many animals with zero, two, four, six, or eight legs as they can.

Imagine scientists have discovered a new animal species. Write a description and draw a picture of the animal. Don't forget to give it a cool name!

How Do Chameleons Change Color?

WITH EYES THAT CAN LOOK IN two different directions at once and sticky, bug-catching tongues, chameleons are incredible creatures. But these reptiles are most famous for their ability to change color.

Most animals have special cells in their skin that contain *pigments*, or substances that give the skin its color. Chameleons have several layers of these cells, each with different pigments. One of these layers also contains tiny crystals that reflect light. Chameleons can control how much distance there is between these crystals and pigments. Changing the distance alters the way light is reflected through the various pigment layers. And this can change the colors that appear on the reptile's skin.

For example, when a chameleon is relaxed, its skin color is usually blue or green. When a chameleon is excited, the reptile can expand its skin cells to increase the distance between the crystals and pigments. This causes its skin to turn colors such as yellow, orange, and red.

All of this color-changing helps make chameleons master communicators. They change hues to "talk" to each other. Certain colors may attract mates or warn other chameleons to back off their territory. Changing color also helps chameleons control their body temperature. Certain colors absorb more heat, which helps keep a chameleon warm; others reflect light away, cooling down the reptile. Now that's brilliant.

WARMING UP WITH COLOR

Which colors might help a chameleon warm up and which ones could help it cool off? Do this experiment to find out.

You Need

- Table
- 5 identical glass jars or drinking glasses
- White, black, blue, red, and green construction paper
- Tape
- Pitcher of water
- Kitchen thermometer

1. Set up a table in a sunny spot outside. Put all your supplies on the table.

2. Wrap a different-colored piece of construction paper around each jar or glass. Use tape to hold it in place.

3. Pour the same amount of water in each jar or glass.

4. Measure the temperature of the water in each jar or glass. They should be the same.

5. Leave the jars or glasses outside on the table to soak up the sun.

6. Return a few hours later. Measure the temperature of the water in each jar or glass. Are the temperatures still the same?

How It Works:

Different colors absorb and reflect the sun's energy in different ways. Dark surfaces absorb more light and heat. Lighter surfaces reflect more light and heat. This is why you feel cooler when you wear lighter colors on hot summer days. Chameleons can't change clothes, but they can regulate their body temperature in another way. When the temperature is cold, they may turn a darker color to absorb more heat. When it's warm, they may turn lighter colors so they can reflect heat and stay cool.

COLORFUL GAMES

Chameleons use colors to communicate, and so do humans. Our brains have even been trained to interpret colors in a specific way. What happens if the rules change? Communicate with friends using colors and then see how colors can trick your brain!

RED LIGHT, GREEN LIGHT

Try this classic game with a twist!

1. Think about a traffic light. Talk with your friends about what the colors on the traffic light mean (red = stop; green = go; yellow = yield).

2. Switch up the rules! Now, red = go; green = stop; yellow = move forward . . . but hop!

3. Play red light, green light. Go outside. One person is the caller. Everyone else stands in a line far away. When the caller says, "Red light," everyone moves forward. When the caller says, "Green light," everyone stops. If the caller says, "Yellow light," players hop forward. People who don't follow directions are out. The first person to reach the caller wins.

COLOR BRAINTEASER

Will you be fooled by these color swaps?

You Need

- Crayons or pieces of colored paper (blue, green, yellow, brown, gray, pink, black, white, red, purple, beige, orange)
- Stopwatch

1. Organize the crayons or pieces of colored paper in rows. Name each color as quickly as you can. Have a friend keep time with a stopwatch.

2. Look at the brainteaser below. Name each color as quickly as you can. How many colors did you name correctly? How long did it take to get them all right? Compare your times from step 1 and step 2.

How It Works: Words have meaning. Colors do, too. When the words and colors are mismatched, it takes your brain longer to get everything right. ■

How Do Flamingos Balance on One Leg?

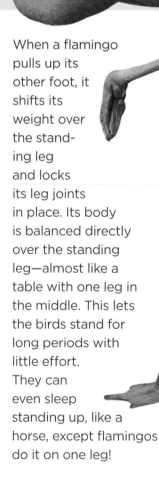

YOU CAN PROBABLY BALANCE on one leg without much trouble. But how about standing on one leg for hours at a time? Most people couldn't do this. For flamingos, it's not a challenge.

Scientists have found that flamingos are able to balance on one leg easily thanks to the way their bodies are built. If you look at a flamingo leg, it seems very long with a knee in the middle and a small foot at the bottom. But that "knee" in the middle is actually a flamingo's ankle, and the "foot" is its toes. That means a flamingo is balancing on a tiptoe.

Although this standing position would be tricky for humans, its actually one of the most balanced positions a flamingo can stand in.

When a flamingo pulls up its other foot, it shifts its weight over the standing leg and locks its leg joints in place. Its body is balanced directly over the standing leg—almost like a table with one leg in the middle. This lets the birds stand for long periods with little effort. They can even sleep standing up, like a horse, except flamingos do it on one leg!

BALANCE CHALLENGES

Make like a flamingo and test your balance with these fun activities.

You Need

- Wall to lean against
- Partner
- Pencil
- Chair (straight back, no armrests)

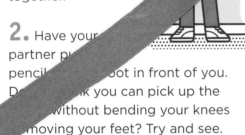

CHALLENGE 1

1. Stand with your back against the wall. Make sure your heels are touching the wall and your feet are together.

2. Have your partner p... penci... ...ot in front of you. D... ...k you can pick up the ... without bending your knees ...moving your feet? Try and see.

3. Stand away from the wall and try again. Compare the results.

CHALLENGE 2

1. Stand tall, away from the wall, with both feet on the ground. You can bend your knees, but hold your arms tight against the sides of your body. Can you lift your left foot without moving your right foot? Try and see.

2. N... stand with your right side—f... hip, arm, and shoulder—against ... wall. Try again. Compare the results.

CHALLENGE 3

1. Sit up straight on the edge of the chair with your feet flat on the ground and your hands on your thighs. Can you stand up—keeping your back straight, your feet flat on the floor, and your hands on your thighs? Try and see.

2. Try again, but lean forward this time. Compare the results.

How It Works:
Solid objects, including people, have a center of mass. When it's in balance, so are we. When it moves—like when you bend forward—you must move, too, in order to keep your mass centered and regain your balance. When it's not allowed to move (as in the chair experiment), you're stuck, too!

BALANCE A FLAMINGO ON ONE LEG

Create a flamingo sculpture
that balances on one leg.

- Paper
- Pencil
- Colored pencils
- Scissors
- Tall, thin bottle with a cap
- Water
- Toothpicks
- 1 large marshmallow
- 4 pipe cleaners
- Handful of round cereal with
  a hole in the middle, such as
  Cheerios or Fruit Loops

1. Trace this flamingo onto the
paper with your pencil. Then
color it in and cut it out.

2. Fill the bottle with
water and screw
on the cap.

3. Stick one toothpick into
the middle of the bottom end
of the large marshmallow.

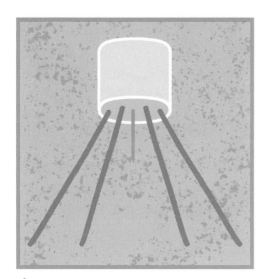

4. Stick four pipe cleaners around the edges of the marshmallow's bottom, angling them out to create a tent.

5. Place your flamingo on the top of the marshmallow. Poke a toothpick through the body of your flamingo. Then push the bottom of this toothpick into the top of the marshmallow so the flamingo rests on top of it.

6. Add an equal number of cereal pieces to the end of each pipe cleaner. These pieces act as weights. Bend the end of each pipe cleaner to hold the cereal in place.

7. Place the bottom toothpick in the large marshmallow on top of the bottle cap. Can you make the flamingo balance on one leg? If not, adjust the weights or bend the pipe cleaners until it does.

How It Works:
To tackle this experiment, the flamingo's center of gravity has to be, well, in the center! To accomplish this, you must distribute the weight equally on all four sides. A flamingo's body is built to master this trick. Its anatomy allows the flamingo to distribute its weight, which helps the bird achieve one-footed balance for long periods of time. ■

More Ideas

Make the length of the central toothpick shorter or longer. How does this affect the flamingo's balance? Make the four angled pipe cleaners different lengths. How does this affect the distribution of the weights?

How Do Dogs' Noses Pick Up So Many Scents?

SCIENTISTS HAVE FOUND THAT some dogs can smell up to 100,000 times better than humans. This is because of the many differences between a dog nose and a human nose.

Tiny cells called *olfactory receptors* line the insides of both dog and human noses. The receptors react to scent molecules and send information to the brain. A dog has many more olfactory receptors than a human. And a dog's receptors have many more tiny hairs, called *cilia*, which allow the animal to detect odors. What's more, the part of a dog's brain that detects odors is much larger compared to a human's. This combination of features heightens a dog's smelling abilities.

In addition to having more olfactory cells, the anatomy of a dog's nose makes it ideal for sniffing. A dog has a large space located deep in its nose that is lined with olfactory receptors. When a dog is detecting odors, it breathes in and out, or sniffs, rapidly. This quick sniffing allows a dog to constantly inhale air and expose its olfactory cells to scents. A dog can also sniff through each side of its nose separately, allowing the dog to pinpoint particular scents.

To top it all off, dogs have a special organ for smelling. This organ is called the *vomeronasal organ*. It is used to detect chemicals that signal changes in a dog's behavior, which is important when socializing with other dogs. Altogether, this special nose makes dogs super smellers.

SCENT MATCHING GAME

In just a few minutes, you can create a sensory smelling game with a few ingredients and a blindfold.

You Need

- Paper cups
- Items with different odors, such as pickles, onions, coffee grounds, hand lotion, shampoo, various fruits, or toast
- Parchment paper
- Tape
- Sharp pencil
- Blindfold

FOR TWO SCIENTISTS

1. Line six cups up in a row. Number the cups 1–6. Place one item in each cup.

2. Make another row of numbered cups. Fill these cups with the same items.

3. Cover the top of the cups with parchment paper. Tape around the edges so the paper is secure. Poke a few holes in the paper with the pencil.

4. Have a friend slide the cups around so they are mixed up. Don't peek!

5. Put on a blindfold. Pick up the cups one by one and smell the contents. Try to match each cup with its partner. ■

More Ideas

Fill six cups with different objects and have your blindfolded partner smell them. Then switch out some of the cups. Wait a couple minutes. Have your partner do the test again and see if they can sniff out which scents are new.

How Do Snakes Slither?

IMAGINE TRYING TO CRAWL forward on your belly without using arms or legs. For snakes, this is a reality—except that snakes have some special adaptations to help them out.

Unlike people, snakes have scales. These scales are made of *keratin*—the same material that makes up your hair and fingernails. A snake uses the tough scales on its belly to grip the ground and drag itself forward. Scientists also recently discovered a new part of snakes' scales that helps them move: a fatty oil that allows them to glide smoothly.

Additionally, snakes have more bones in their spines than people do. Most humans only have 33 vertebrae (spine bones) and 24 ribs. A snake has between 200 and 400 vertebrae, and just as many ribs. This makes snakes very flexible. It also means that they have lots of muscles along their bellies, connected to their many ribs. Snakes rely on these muscles to help push themselves along the ground. Most snakes push first on one side of their bodies, and then on the other. This creates their famous winding slither.

Sometimes though, bigger snakes, such as boa constrictors, move forward in a straight line. To do this, a snake will pull the front half of its body forward, then drag the back half forward to meet it—sort of like an accordion.

SCALING STRAIGHT UP!

It's one thing for a snake to drag itself across the ground. But how does an animal with no legs defy gravity to pull itself up trees? As when they are on the ground, snakes use their muscles and scales to grip a tree's bark. But here, they take things up a notch—some snakes can angle their scales outward for a better grip on the bark, and some can use their muscles to grip the tree extra hard. If a tree branch is small enough, a snake will also often wind itself around the branch to get a better hold. Or, if the tree is large enough, a snake can find crevices in the bark that give it hand-holds—well, snakeholds.

BUILD A BUBBLE SNAKE

Want to watch a snake slither? Okay, this isn't a real snake—it's made of bubbles. But you'll still be impressed with its moves!

You Need

- Safety goggles
- Clear plastic water bottle
- Scissors
- Long, thin sock
- Rubber band (optional)
- Bowl
- ¼ cup dish soap
- ½ cup water
- Liquid food coloring (optional)
- Ruler

1. Put on your safety goggles.

2. Take the lid off the plastic bottle. With an adult's help, use scissors to cut the bottom off the bottle.

3. From the bottom up, slide a sock over the rest of the water bottle. Fold the sock down so it fits snugly. If it's a little loose, secure it with a rubber band. This completes your bubble machine.

4. Prepare the bubble mix. Pour the water and dish soap into the bowl. Swirl gently.

5. Dip the bubble machine into the bubble mix, sock end first.

6. Take the bottle out of the bubble mix and blow through the top of the bottle. Blow again and again. Watch your bubble snake grow.

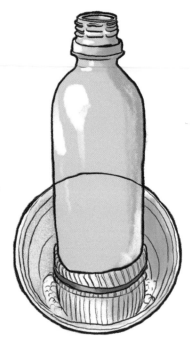

7. Have a friend record how long your snake grows before it breaks.

How It Works:

When you exhale, you breathe out a mixture of gases. The bubble solution traps these gases when you blow. And the tiny holes in the sock create many tiny bubbles all at once, forming a chain. The more you blow, the more gases you exhale, and the longer your snake grows. ∎

More Ideas

For a more colorful bubble snake, decorate the end of the sock with food coloring before dipping it into the bubble mix. Use different colors to create amazing patterns. You can see the patterns better if you use a white sock.

How Do Animals Hibernate?

DO YOU EVER WISH YOU COULD slow down and snuggle up throughout the cold months of the year? That's just what some animals do during the winter!

To get through the cold winter months when food is scarce, some animals enter a state of hibernation. This is when an animal saves energy by slowing down a lot of its bodily functions.

Animals are not always asleep when they hibernate. Though during hibernation, an animal's breathing, heart, body temperature, and digestion rates will all lower by a lot. This allows an animal to survive for long periods of time without eating or drinking, as they are using much less energy.

As temperatures drop, animals prepare for hibernation by eating as much food as they can or by storing food nearby for the brief times when they're awake. Once the weather becomes cold, it triggers the animals' bodies to slow down. Some animals hibernate for up to 150 days. During this time, most of them live off the fat and nutrients stored in their bodies. As the seasons warm, the animals' bodies will start to return to normal, until—rise and shine!—they return to being active.

HEART RATE INVESTIGATION

A hibernating animal's heart rate is super slow. When you sit around, your heart rate is slow, too. So what happens to your heart rate when you start moving? It's time to get sweaty to find out!

You Need

- Piece of paper
- Pen or pencil
- Stopwatch
- Simple exercise equipment, such as jump rope, bicycle, light weights, etc.

1. Find your pulse. Use the first two fingers of one hand to feel your radial pulse on the inside of your other wrist. Practice until you can find your pulse quickly.

2. Lie still for several minutes. Then take your pulse for 15 seconds. Multiply the number by four. This is your resting heart rate in beats per minute. Write it down on your paper.

3. Create a six-column chart on your paper. Label the columns as follows: *Exercise, 1 minute, 2 minutes, 5 minutes, 10 minutes, and 15 minutes.*

4. Decide which exercises you will do. Some exercises, like jumping rope or riding a bike, will require equipment. Others, like walking or skipping, will not. Gather any equipment you need.

5. Starting at a resting heart rate, begin your first exercise. Stop after 1, 2, 5, 10, and 15 minutes of activity. Take your pulse for 15 seconds each time. Record the numbers on your chart. Multiply them by four.

6. Relax until you are back to your resting heart rate.

7. Repeat with one or two other exercises. Examine the results. ■

Did You Know?

Heart rate can vary by age. For newborns, a healthy resting heart rate is between 70 and 190 beats per minute. For anyone over the age of 10, it's 60 to 100 beats per minute.

How Do Cats Land on Their Feet?

HAVE YOU EVER HEARD THE saying "Cats always land on their feet?" While cats don't land on their feet every time, they do have an amazing ability to right themselves during a fall. There's even a name for it: the *righting reflex*.

Most animals have a righting reflex, but cats do it best, especially when in the air. Cats have more vertebrae in their spines than humans do, as well as extra-elastic tissue in between. This makes their backs very flexible. They also have small collar bones and shoulder blades (the triangle-shaped bones in the upper back) that are only attached by muscles as opposed to bone. Altogether, this makes cats able to

twist and bend in ways that humans can't. Cats (and people) rely on small organs in their ears, known as the *vestibular system*, to keep their balance. When they begin to fall, the vestibular system tells cats which way is up and which way is down. They then use their flexible backs to twist in midair so that their feet are facing the ground.

Scientists think that some cats might also help slow their fall by stretching out their bodies midair. The stretched-out body might act as a sort of parachute, slowing them down for a softer landing. All in all, cats land on their feet because they are designed to be furry acrobats!

Safety Tip

Never drop a cat—they can still get hurt during a fall.

NIGHT VISION

Cats don't just have an amazing set of reflexes—they can also see much better in the dark than we can thanks to their unique eyes. Cats, like many other animals that hunt at night, have a special reflective structure in their eyes called a *tapetum lucidum*. This sends more light to the cells in their eyes that process vision. They also have slit-shaped pupils, unlike our round ones. These can expand larger than ours to let in even more light.

FINDING GRAVITY

So why do cats fall DOWN every time after they jump UP? Gravity! You can't see gravity, but with these simple experiments, you can prove it exists.

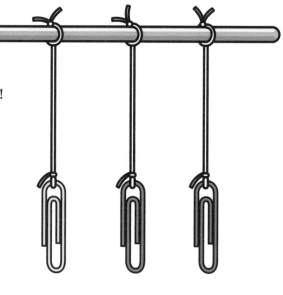

GRAVITY'S PULL

You Need

- Stick
- 3 paper clips
- 3 pieces of string

1. Tie one end of a piece of string to a paper clip. Tie the other end of the string around one end of the stick.

2. Repeat twice. Space the strings out on the stick.

3. Hold the stick level in the air. Observe how the strings hang.

4. Tilt the stick one way and then the other. See how the strings hang now.

How It Works:
No matter which way the stick is tilted, the paper clips always point straight toward the ground. You can thank gravity for this. *Gravity* is the force that pulls objects toward Earth's center. Even when the stick is tilted, gravity pulls the paper clips straight toward Earth.

CENTER OF GRAVITY

You Need

- Pencil
- Pencil top eraser

1. Try to balance a pencil on your finger. Keep trying until you find the point where it doesn't fall off.

2. Put an eraser on the end of the pencil. Try again.

How It Works:
When you can balance the pencil, you have found the pencil's center of gravity. The weight on each side of this point is equal. When you add the eraser, you add weight. You have to find the new center of gravity.

GALILEO'S EXPERIMENT

You Need

- Small unbreakable toy
- Pencil
- Sturdy chair
- Various items of different shapes and sizes
- Piece of paper

1. Observe the toy and the pencil. If you dropped them at the same time, which item do you think would hit the ground first?

2. Ask an adult to stand nearby, or hold on to the chair. Stand on the chair, holding the toy in one hand and the pencil in the other.

3. Drop the items at the same time. Observe the results.

4. Try again, testing two other items. What happened?

5. Repeat the test using the piece of paper and the toy. What happened now?

How It Works:
Earth's gravity pulls on all objects the same, regardless of how much they weigh. That's why most items hit the ground at the same time. With the paper, another force comes into play. Air resistance pushes against the paper, causing it to fall at a slower rate. Imagine that the piece of paper was a parachute. How does air resistance keep skydivers safe?

FALLING WATER

You Need

- Paper cup
- Pencil
- Water

1. Go outside. This experiment can get messy!

2. Poke a hole in the bottom of the cup with the pencil.

3. Cover the hole with your finger. Then fill the cup with water.

4. Remove your finger. Watch how the water trickles out.

5. Repeat step 3.

6. Remove your finger as you drop the cup to the ground. What happens to the water?

How It Works:
When you held the cup, gravity pulled water toward the ground and water pressure forced it out of the hole. When you dropped the cup, the cup and water fell at the same speed because they were pulled on by the same force of gravity. Because everything was falling at the same time, there was no pressure to force water from the hole. ∎

How Do Bats Navigate in the Dark?

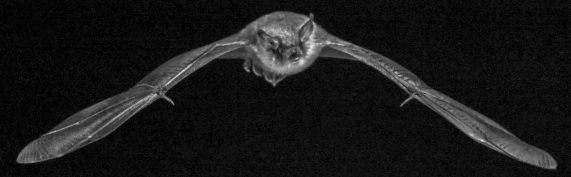

IF SOMEONE IS HAVING TROUBLE seeing, they might say that they're "as blind as a bat." Bats aren't actually blind. But the saying does have some truth to it, in that most bats don't rely on their vision to fly around and catch bugs in the dark.

Instead, bats use something called *echolocation*. To echolocate, an animal sends out very high-pitched sounds. The animal then listens for any echoes as the sounds bounce off objects. By listening to these echoes, a bat can tell not only where the object is, but how big it is and what its shape is. In fact, bats can sense an object as thin as a strand of human hair by using echolocation. Maybe the saying should be "as talented as a bat!"

OTHER ANIMAL ECHOLOCATORS

Bats aren't the only animals that echolocate—check out some other members of the animal kingdom with this fantastic skill.

DOLPHINS
Dolphins use a special sound-making organ located near their blowholes to echolocate. Like bats, dolphins use echolocation to hunt and navigate.

SHREWS
Scientists have found that shrews have very poor eyesight. Instead of using their sense of sight to get around, they likely rely on echolocation to find their way through their underground burrows.

HUMANS
It may come as a surprise, but there are some people who have trained themselves to echolocate! In fact, scientists are studying how people with impaired vision can use echolocation to help navigate the world.

ECHOLOCATION EXPERIMENT

Get a little batty and talk to your friends with this echolocation device!

You Need

- 2 empty paper towel tubes
- Table
- Square aluminum pan
- Rulers
- Masking tape
- Books (optional)

FOR TWO SCIENTISTS

1. Tape two paper towel tubes to the table. The tubes should be no more than two inches apart, and they should be angled toward each other but not touching.

2. Place the square pan upright so the deep part is facing the tubes. It should be at least 12 inches from the tubes. Use tape or books to secure the pan in place.

3. Whisper a word into your tube. Have your partner listen for the sound of your word through their tube. Try again.

4. Switch roles. Listen for the sounds of your partner's words.

How It Works:

When you make a sound, it travels through the air. Your tube directs that sound toward the pan. When the sound hits the pan, it bounces back toward the other tube. This is how echolocation works. Echolocation helps animals like bats avoid crashing into things. It also helps them find food and avoid predators. ■

More Ideas

Use the tubes to try to bounce sound off walls, doors, and other solid surfaces. Make sure the tubes are at an angle and at least a foot away from the solid surface.

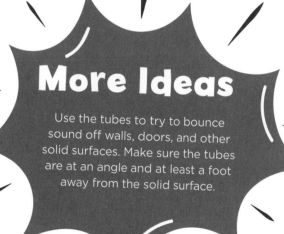

How Does a Whale's Blowhole Work?

LIKE YOU, WHALES CAN'T breathe underwater. Also like you, they breathe in and out through an opening. But whales don't breathe through noses and mouths as humans do—instead, they take in air through the tops of their heads!

A whale's blowhole allows the whale to take quick breaths of air while remaining mostly underwater. After breathing in, they can hold their breath for long amounts of time. This is because, unlike humans, they don't need to store all their air in their lungs. Whales can also store oxygen in their blood and muscles. They can also slow down the functions of many of their organs, meaning that they use less air over time.

When a whale is ready to exhale, it returns to the surface. It then exhales a huge burst of air (and sometimes snot!) back through its blowhole. This air can sometimes send water flying as well, which is why it often looks like a whale is shooting water from its blowhole. Then, the whale is ready to take another breath and dive back down.

Close-up of a Blowhole

Did You Know?

When a whale exhales, its breath is warm. As this warm breath comes into contact with the cold air around it, the moisture in the air condenses, forming droplets. This enhances the illusion that a whale is shooting water from its blowhole.

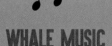

WHALE MUSIC

Whales communicate through lots of different sounds, from clicks to whistles. But some whales, like humpbacks and blue whales, sing! Like humans, these whales have vocal cords that let them make a variety of sounds. But unlike humans, they also have special sacs in their throats. Scientists think that this might let whales sing underwater without losing any air.

MAKE A WATERSPOUT

Whales only look like they're spouting water directly from
their blowholes into the air. You can create a real waterspout
using air pressure!

You Need

- 2-liter plastic bottle
- Ruler
- Marker
- Scissors
- Straw
- Modeling clay
- Water
- Large bowl
- Balloon

1. Measure five inches up from the
bottom of the bottle. Make a dot
with the marker.

2. Use scissors to make a hole, just
large enough to fit the straw, where
the dot is.

3. Insert the straw into the hole.
Use modeling clay to seal the hole
around the straw.

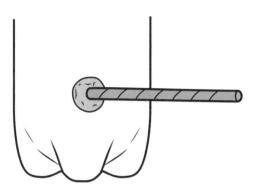

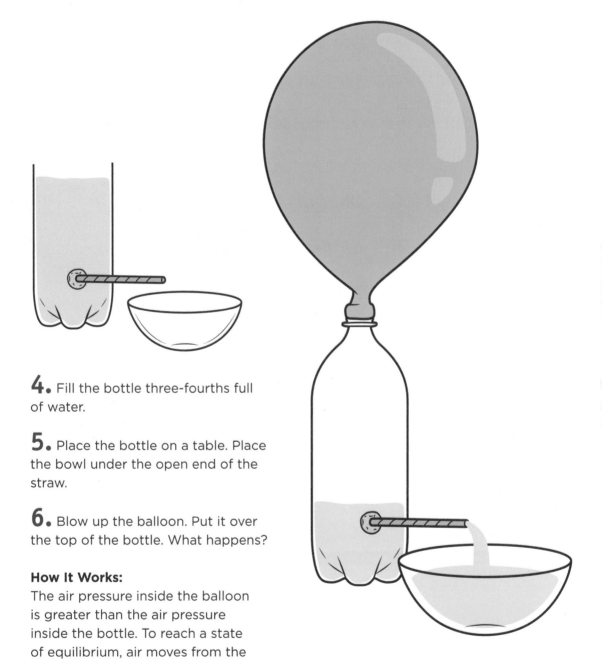

4. Fill the bottle three-fourths full of water.

5. Place the bottle on a table. Place the bowl under the open end of the straw.

6. Blow up the balloon. Put it over the top of the bottle. What happens?

How It Works:
The air pressure inside the balloon is greater than the air pressure inside the bottle. To reach a state of equilibrium, air moves from the balloon into the bottle. This forces water out through the straw. ■

How Do Butterflies Communicate?

HAVE YOU EVER HEARD A butterfly buzz, squeak, or quack? Probably not—that's because most butterflies don't make sounds the way many other animals do.

Many species of butterfly don't make much noise at all. That means most butterflies need to communicate without sound. Instead, they rely on such things as colors, chemicals, and body movements.

To us, a butterfly's colorful wings look beautiful. To another butterfly, those wings hold lots of information, like whether that butterfly is male or female. Butterflies also have compound eyes and can detect many more colors and patterns

BECOMING A BUTTERFLY

Before they can fly, butterflies begin as caterpillars that crawl. To turn themselves into butterflies, some caterpillars molt—or shed—their skin until they harden into what is known as a chrysalis. Other butterflies spin their own chrysalis around themselves. This chrysalis then acts as a cocoon, protecting the animal while special substances in its body, called enzymes, turn the caterpillar into a type of soupy goo. The goo then rebuilds over time into a different shape: that of a butterfly, which emerges from the chrysalis.

than we can. In addition, butterflies can put out and sense chemicals that let them communicate with each other.

Or, if the situation calls for it, butterflies can change up their posture or flying patterns. This can help a butterfly find a partner or tell another butterfly to back off!

However, there are butterflies that do rely on sound. Some butterflies can use their wings to make noises loud enough for humans to hear. Others make very soft clicking noises.

So, while you may never hear a butterfly buzz, if you listen very carefully, you might hear one click.

PLANT A BUTTERFLY GARDEN

Butterflies are beautiful insects. They're also great pollinators. Planting a butterfly garden is a great way to encourage butterflies to visit your yard or even your balcony, roof, or other outdoor space.

You Need

- A good location
- Various flowers, trees, and shrubs that are native to your area
- Large, flat rocks
- Bird bath (optional)
- Soil
- Sand (optional)
- Shovels
- Trowels
- Water
- Pencil and paper

1. **Make a plan.** A successful butterfly garden begins with making good decisions.

2. **Pick the right location.** Choose a spot that gets at least six hours of sunlight a day and provides shelter from the wind. If you have a plot in the ground, make sure it's a chemical-free zone. Pesticides are dangerous for butterflies. If you don't have a plot, you can also create a butterfly garden using a collection of containers on a patio.

3. **Pick the right plants for butterflies.** Adult butterflies drink nectar from flowers. They are attracted to red, yellow, orange, pink, and purple blooms with wide, flat clusters or large, flat petals. Research and choose plants that grow well and are native to where you live.

4. **Pick the right plants for caterpillars.** Caterpillars eat other plant parts. They are picky eaters. Each species eats specific kinds of plants. Butterflies usually lay eggs on the plants their caterpillars eat. For example, monarch butterflies lay their eggs only on milkweed plants.

5. **Draw your idea.** Include trees and shrubs for shelter. Add big flat rocks so butterflies have a place to rest. Include a bird bath or spot with wet sand or soil so they have a place to drink water. Clump flowers of the same kind together so butterflies can see them from a distance. What else would your dream butterfly garden include?

6. **Review your garden plan with a grown-up.** When you're ready, get to work! ■

More Ideas

Plant flowers that bloom at different times so butterflies have a food source all summer long. If you're building a butterfly garden on a patio, position the plants against a fence or a railing for shelter.

DIGGING UP
DINOSAURS

Quick Challenges

Imagine you discovered a new species of dinosaur in your backyard. Come up with a name for it. Imagine what it did and where it lived.

Use different kinds of pasta to build the fossilized skeleton of your favorite dinosaur.

Some dinosaurs ate plants and others ate meat. Make a list of modern-day animals that eat plants or meat.

Make a list of real dinosaurs and made-up ones. Read the list aloud to a friend or family member and see if they can guess which are the actual dinosaurs.

Write a quiz about dinosaurs. Challenge a friend to ace your quiz.

Study some dinosaur names. Then challenge your friends to a dinosaur spelling bee.

How Do We Know About Dinosaurs?

MILLIONS OF YEARS AGO, enormous reptiles roamed Earth. We know this because even though most dinosaurs died long ago (see page 102), they left behind evidence of their existence, known as *fossils*.

Fossils are the remains of plants and animals that lived in the past. Lots of things can turn into fossils, including shells, leaves, feathers, animal bones, and teeth. The most famous type of fossil is called a *body fossil*. When a dinosaur died, it was sometimes quickly buried by mud or sand. Over thousands and thousands of years, this mud and sand turned to rock. Most of the soft body parts of the animal, such as organs, muscle, and

skin, decomposed, but hard bits, such as teeth, bones, and horns, remained. Over time, minerals from sand, mud, and water replaced the hard bits that were left behind. During this process, they became fossils.

Not all fossils are made of bones or teeth. Some fossils, known as *trace fossils*, don't contain any parts of the dinosaur itself. Instead, they contain evidence of dinosaur behavior when the animal was alive, like footprints or burrows. Other times, body parts like feathers, bones, or shells decompose but leave impressions in soft sand that then hardens.When these impressions are filled in with

Continued on next page

Fossil of an Extinct Marine Arthropod

other minerals from the sand or water, they are called *cast fossils*. When these impressions remain hollow and are not filled in with other minerals, they are called mold fossils. Sometimes small lizards, insects, or plants got stuck in sticky tree sap that hardened over time, which might result in an amber fossil.

People have been finding dinosaur fossils for thousands of years. Long ago, people thought the fossils belonged to dragons! It wasn't until the 1800s that scientists studying these fossils began to understand that they were long-extinct reptiles. Scientists who specialize in studying fossils are called *paleontologists*.

HOW DO WE KNOW WHAT COLOR DINOSAURS WERE?

Fossils can tell us lots of things, like what dinosaurs looked like, how big they were, what they ate, and when and where they lived. Recently, paleontologists have even learned from fossils that many dinosaurs had feathers. But some things, like color, are a little trickier to tell. Most of the time, scientists can only guess at what color a dinosaur was. But sometimes, paleontologists get lucky. Inside a dinosaur's feathers and skin—and inside your skin, too!—are special cells called *melanosomes* that make color. Fossilized feathers from certain birds and dinosaurs have let scientists study these cells and determine what color feathers probably were. Skin can be trickier, as it doesn't often fossilize like feathers and bones. Instead, dinosaur skin was preserved as impressions in sand, telling us much about the scaly shape and texture of dinosaur skin but little about its color. But experts are searching hard for fossilized dinosaur skin. Soon, we might know the color of that, too!

Eotrachodon, a Type of Duck-Billed Dinosaur

CREATE FOSSILIZED PRINTS

Use this salt dough recipe to make your own fossils!

You Need

- 1 cup salt
- 2 cups flour
- 1½ cups damp, used coffee grounds
- ¾ cup cold coffee
- Brown food coloring (optional)
- Large mixing bowl
- Spoon
- Paper plates
- Small plastic dinosaurs (optional)

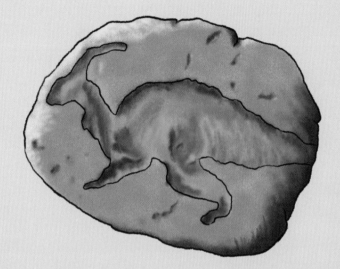

1. Mix the salt, flour, and damp coffee grounds in the bowl with a spoon. Add the coffee a little at a time until you have a thick dough. If you want your "dirt" to be even darker, add a few drops of brown food coloring.

2. Knead the dough with your hands until it is smooth. Add more flour if the dough is too sticky. Add more water if it is too dry.

3. Divide the dough into several pieces. Roll one piece into a ball. Flatten the ball into a disc with your hands. Put it on a paper plate.

4. Roll and flatten the other pieces of dough. Put each piece on a paper plate.

5. Press your fingers, hand, plastic dinosaurs, or other items of your choice into the discs to make prints.

6. Set the paper plates in a warm, dry place. Let the prints dry for several days.

MAKE FOSSILS OUT OF GLUE

Have you ever seen a dinosaur fossil in a museum? Guess what!
It might not have been the real thing. Museums often display cast
fossils, which are 3-D duplicates made from molds of actual fossils.
This simple activity will show you how cast fossils are made.

You Need

- Modeling clay
- Items found in nature, such as seashells, leaves, twigs, blades of grass, etc.
- White glue

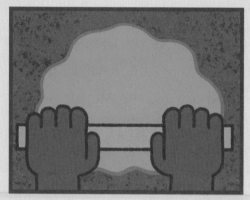

1. Roll, soften, and flatten a piece of modeling clay into a disc.

2. Press natural objects, like seashells, leaves, twigs, or grass, into the clay.

3. Remove the items. Examine your fossil molds. Then fill the shapes with white glue.

4. Let the glue dry for at least 24 hours.

5. Remove the glue shapes from the clay. Examine the cast fossils you made. ■

Tip

Don't press too hard when you create the fossil mold. The glue will dry better and more quickly if the mold is not too deep.

Did You Know

SUE, the most complete *T. rex* fossil ever found, is on display at the Field Museum in Chicago, Illinois. The skull set on the skeleton is a cast, but the real 600-pound skull is on display in a special case nearby.

How Did the Dinosaurs Go Extinct?

SOME 66 MILLION YEARS AGO, dinosaurs ruled the planet. Then, rather suddenly, almost all of them died. What could have caused such a huge extinction event? Scientists aren't 100 percent sure, but they have several ideas that might explain what happened.

One theory that most scientists believe is that about 66 million years ago, a huge space rock—either an asteroid or a comet—crashed into Earth. In 1978, scientists discovered an enormous crater off Mexico's Yucatán Peninsula. They believe that this is where the asteroid or comet—going tens of thousands of miles an hour—struck. An impact of that size and speed would have caused a huge chain reaction around the world, creating everything from tsunamis to volcanic eruptions to wildfires. It also would have caused a cloud of ash and dust to cover the planet.

The ash and dust cloud was likely so thick that it blocked out the sun for long periods at a time. Temperatures around Earth probably plummeted, making it too cold for dinosaurs. What's more, sources of food for dinosaurs were wiped out in these harsh conditions. Scientists believe that over the course of 10,000 years after the space rock struck, almost all the dinosaurs went extinct.

AFTER THE DINOSAURS

Did you know that not all dinosaurs went extinct? In fact, you've probably seen lots of dinosaurs. That's because all birds, from the tiniest hummingbird to the largest eagle, are considered living dinosaurs—more specifically, *avian dinosaurs*. About 150 million years ago, avian dinosaurs, which evolved from small meat-eating dinosaurs, began to appear. These were dinosaurs that had feathers and most could fly. When the space rock struck, all of the nonavian dinosaurs died.

But the avian dinosaurs lived on! Over time, they evolved into the modern avian dinosaurs—that is to say, the birds—we're familiar with today.

IMPACT CRATER EXPERIMENT

The space rock that hit Earth and led to the extinction of most dinosaurs created a massive crater in the ground. It measures between 110 and 150 miles wide. Mostly buried beneath limestone now, scientists think the crater was up to 3,000 feet deep at the moment of impact. Find out how craters are formed with this experiment.

You Need

- Old newspapers or old sheet, to protect your work area
- Large shallow pan or tray with edges
- Flour
- Sifter or sieve
- Colored powder, such as dry pudding mix or cocoa powder
- Small objects of various shapes and sizes to use as meteors, such as marbles, table tennis balls, marshmallows, raisins, buttons, or seeds
- Ruler
- Paper
- Pencil

1. Cover your work area with old newspapers.

2. Place a large tray or pan on top of the newspapers. Fill the tray or pan with one or two inches of flour. Make the layer as smooth as possible.

3. Using the sifter or sieve, add a thin layer of colored powder on top of the flour.

4. Select one round object to use as your first meteor. Hold it a few feet above the tray or pan. Predict what will happen to the flour surface when you drop it.

5. Drop the object and observe. Measure and record the width of the crater. Draw a picture to show what it looks like.

6. Drop the object from a higher point so it is traveling faster when it hits the surface. Drop it from a lower height so it is traveling slower. Drop it from a different angle. Compare the results.

7. Drop objects of different sizes and shapes. Compare the results. How do size, shape, speed, and angle affect the size and shape of craters when a meteorite hits the surface? ■

Tip
To get the best results, refresh your testing surface between attempts. Use the sifter or sieve to add a small amount of the colored powder you used.

How Did Dinosaurs Care for Their Babies?

AS WITH MANY THINGS concerning dinosaur behavior, scientists can't be completely sure how dinosaur parents cared for their babies. After all, they lived millions of years ago. But studying fossilized dinosaur nests has helped scientists understand more about how dinosaur parents might have acted.

As far as scientists know, all dinosaurs laid eggs. But not all those eggs were the same. Some dinosaurs laid eggs with soft shells, as turtles do. Others laid eggs with hard shells, as modern birds do. Dinosaur eggs also came in different shapes. Some eggs were round like a ball, others were long and oval shaped. Dinosaurs also laid eggs in different places. Some dinosaur parents looked for safe areas on land and laid eggs in nests out in the open or nests hidden by nearby plants. Others dug burrows in sand or mud.

Museum Replica of *Maiasaura* Eggs Hatching

After a female dinosaur laid her eggs, she or another adult dinosaur probably "sat" on the eggs to keep them warm. Scientists think that larger dinosaurs even had special ways of setting up their nests to keep the eggs warm without crushing them: Larger dinosaurs sometimes arranged their eggs in a ring, and then sat in the center of this ring. This may have let them keep the eggs warm or protect them without squishing them.

Once the babies hatched, a dinosaur parent was responsible for feeding them. Scientists aren't sure how dinosaurs did this. They may have brought food back to the nests and left it for their babies. Or they may have chowed down the food themselves, and then thrown it back up for their babies to eat, as birds do.

Based on fossilized nests, scientists also think that dinosaurs stayed around to protect their babies after they hatched.

OVIRAPTOR

In 1922, scientists in Mongolia discovered the fossil of a meat-eating dinosaur near a nest of fossilized eggs. They figured that the dinosaur was a hungry hunter out to snack on some eggs. They named the dinosaur *Oviraptor,* which means "egg stealer." But in 1993, scientists made another discovery: The *Oviraptor* was actually taking care of a nest of *Oviraptor* eggs!

BUBBLY DINOSAUR EGGS

Take a step back in time!
Mix an acid and a base to hatch
your own "baby dinosaurs."

Tip
Wearing dish gloves as you mold the eggs will keep the food coloring from staining your hands. Use multiple colors of dough to create a more colorful egg.

You Need

- Baking soda
- Large bowl
- Water
- Spoons
- Multiple small bowls
- Food coloring
- Dish gloves (optional)
- Small plastic dinosaurs
- Large tray or cookie sheet
- Spray bottle or dropper
- Vinegar or lemon juice
- Baking pan

1. Pour a box of baking soda into a large bowl. Add a small amount of water. Stir. Continue to add just enough extra water to get a damp, doughy mixture.

2. Divide the dough into parts. Put each part in a separate small bowl. Add a few drops of food coloring to each bowl. Stir it in.

3. Grab the dough from one of the bowls. Place a plastic dinosaur in the middle and mold the dough around the dinosaur. Create an egg shape.

4. Repeat step 3 to make more dinosaur eggs.

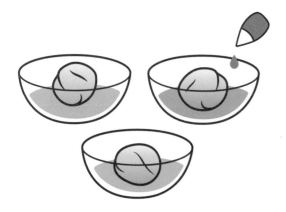

5. Place the finished eggs on a tray or cookie sheet. Freeze the eggs or let them dry overnight. They should be completely dry.

6. The next day, fill the spray bottle or dropper with vinegar or lemon juice. Put one or more eggs in a baking pan. Squirt the eggs with vinegar or lemon juice and watch them fizz away until your dinosaurs hatch!

How It Works:

Vinegar and lemon juice are acids. Baking soda is a base. When you mix an acid and a base together, a chemical reaction occurs, and a new product is created. In this reaction, that new product is carbon dioxide bubbles. ■

How Fast Did T. Rex Run?

IF YOU'VE EVER SEEN A DINOSAUR movie, you've probably thought that *T. rex* must have been pretty fast. After all, movie scenes sometimes show these dinosaurs keeping up with cars! For a long time, paleontologists thought so, too.

Scientists trying to figure out how fast a *T. rex* could run often used computer reconstructions that built digital models based on *T. rex* body fossils. This led them to think that the giant dinosaurs could run about 30 miles per hour. The average adult human can only run about 15 miles per hour at top speed. But recently, scientists have discovered that there may be more to a *T. rex*'s run.

Before, scientists were focusing on the dinosaur's legs and hips. Now, paleontologists are making new computer simulations that also include the tail and account for the dinosaur's muscles, weight, and posture. By scanning a *T. rex* fossil, scientists were able to study a more complete computer model. This model showed that a *T. rex* may have walked at only about 2.9 miles per hour.

As for running, scientists still aren't quite sure. Some scientists think that a *T. rex*'s huge size would have made running difficult, as its bones could break if it moved too quickly. This would put its running speed at about 12 miles per hour. Other scientists think that the dinosaur's heavy tail could have helped it absorb some of the impact of running, letting it sprint up to about 25 miles per hour. Either way, it wouldn't have been winning any races against a car.

T. REX TAILS

Without a living example, it's very difficult for scientists to figure out how dinosaurs might have moved. So, to hopefully figure out how a *T. rex* moved when it walked, scientists turned to one of its closest living relatives: the chicken. To get a better idea of a *T. rex*'s movements, the scientists attached a fake tail to a chicken and filmed how it walked.

ANALYZE FOSSIL FOOTPRINTS

A walking or running *T. rex* can leave quite an impression . . . literally! Scientists have found fossilized footprints from *T. rex* and other dinosaurs around the world. What information might scientists get from footprints? Do this experiment to find out!

You Need

- Old newspapers
- Masking tape
- 3 cookie sheets
- Red, green, and blue finger paint
- Chair
- Tub of soapy water
- Old towel

Safety Tip

Be VERY careful moving across the paper strip in this activity so you don't slip.

1. Ask an adult for permission before doing this activity. If they agree, line up several old newspaper sheets to create one long strip. Tape the papers together and secure them to the floor with tape.

2. Place the cookie sheets at one end of the paper strip. Pour one color of finger paint into each cookie sheet. Place the chair, tub of soapy water, and towel at the other end of the paper strip.

3. Step barefoot into the cookie sheet filled with red finger paint. Make sure the bottoms of your feet are covered with paint. Slowly walk the full length of the paper strip. Be careful not to slip! When you get to the other end, sit in the chair and use the tub of soapy water to clean your feet. Dry your feet with the towel.

4. Repeat step 3 with the other colors. But slowly jog across the paper strip when you use the green paint. Get finger paint on your hands and feet and do a bear crawl across the paper strip when you use the blue finger paint.

5. Compare and contrast the results.

How It Works:
Look closely. When you travel different ways, your footprints leave different patterns. These patterns can show how big you are, how many legs you used, and how you traveled. The layers of footprints even show which way you traveled first. ■

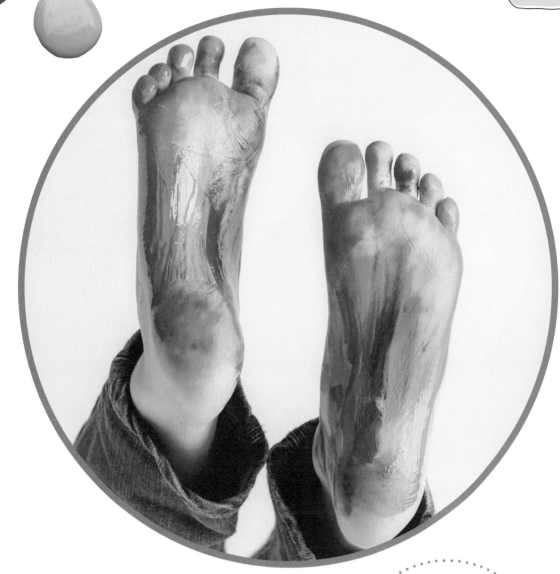

Did You Know ?

A team of paleontologists found 21 different types of dinosaur footprint fossils at a site in Australia. The largest footprint, left by a sauropod, was five feet and nine inches long. It is the biggest dinosaur footprint ever found!

Tip

Wear clothes that are old or that you don't care about getting paint on. If you have on a long-sleeve shirt or pants, roll them up during the activity.

How Did Triceratops Use Its Horns?

TRICERATOPS GETS ITS NAME from its appearance. In Greek, *Triceratops* means "three-horned face." This plant-eating dinosaur is famous for its three horns. It had one above each eye and one on its nose. *Triceratops* also had a distinct-looking neck frill behind its head.

DINO DANCE

Dinosaur suitors may have had another method for showing off to potential mates: dancing. Scientists think that many dinosaurs may have performed dance-like courtship rituals similar to those of many modern birds.

When paleontologists first discovered *Triceratops*, they theorized that these dinosaurs may have used their horns to battle each other or to defend against hungry predators. Since then, scientists have made more discoveries that suggest this might be true. Scientists found one fossil belonging to a *Triceratops* that had part of one horn bitten off, which may have happened as the dinosaur fended off an attack. Other fossils have been found with marks along the horns and frill that make scientists think male *Triceratops* may have battled each other to impress mates.

However, scientists have also recently developed a new theory: A *Triceratops's* horns may have been used to attract mates—without any battling. Similar to how male peacocks impress potential partners with their beautiful feathers, *Triceratops* may have displayed their fancy frills and horns to woo other dinosaurs.

OBSERVE A LIVING DINOSAUR

Even though you can't watch a real *Triceratops* to see how it behaved, there is one kind of living dinosaur you can study—birds!

You Need

- Binoculars
- Notebook
- Pen or pencil

1. Go outside and find a place to study birds. If this isn't possible, with an adult's help, find videos to watch online about birds.

2. Sit as quietly as possible so you don't disturb the birds. Observe each bird closely: How does it move? What does it eat? Does it like to be alone or in a group? How does it act with birds of its own species? How does it act with birds of different species?

Can you see where the bird lives? If so, what does its home look like? Use binoculars to get a closer look.

3. Record the information in your notebook. Record the time, date, and location of each observation. Draw pictures to illustrate your findings.

4. Conduct observations of different kinds of birds over multiple days. Compare two of these birds. How are they the same? How are they different? ■

Tip

Be safe. Always take an adult or a buddy when you study birds in a public place.

American Goldfinch

How Did Dinosaurs Stay Balanced?

SOME DINOSAURS COULD GROW to enormous sizes. It must have been difficult for them to manage so much mass, especially those that walked on two feet. How did they do it?

To stay balanced, all dinosaurs—whether they walked on two legs or four—most likely relied on their tails. This is similar to how many four-legged animals today balance.

Wulatelong, a Bird-Like Dinosaur from Mongolia

For instance, researchers have found that cheetahs use their tails to help keep their balance as they run, and even to turn suddenly.

By relying on computer simulations, scientists have been able to model how many dinosaurs might have moved their tails while they walked. In fact, it seems that many two-legged dinosaurs actually wagged their tails to keep steady while they moved.

A two-legged dinosaur's arms also helped it stay upright. Some two-legged dinosaurs, like *T. rex* and *Carnotaurus sastrei,* evolved to have large heads but very short arms. They likely used these little clawed arms to slash prey for dinner. But short arms may have also helped make these dinosaurs less heavy toward their fronts, which prevented them from toppling over.

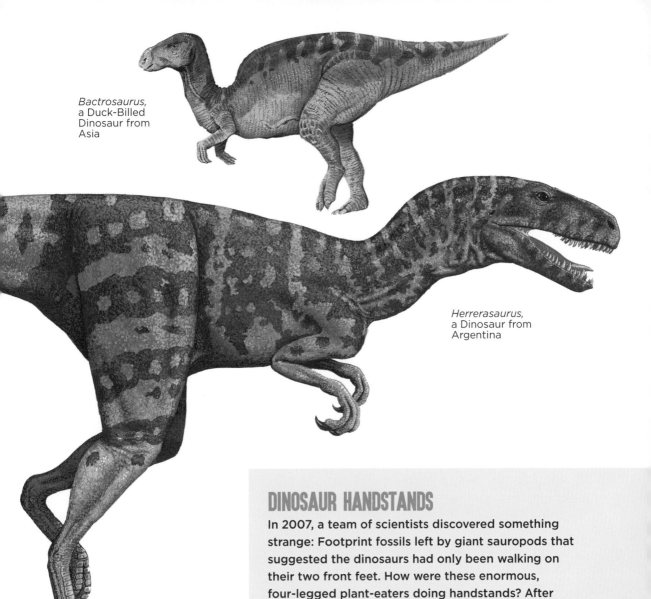

Bactrosaurus, a Duck-Billed Dinosaur from Asia

Herrerasaurus, a Dinosaur from Argentina

DINOSAUR HANDSTANDS

In 2007, a team of scientists discovered something strange: Footprint fossils left by giant sauropods that suggested the dinosaurs had only been walking on their two front feet. How were these enormous, four-legged plant-eaters doing handstands? After lots of analysis, the scientists think they have an answer: The dinosaurs were using their front feet to wade in shallow water while their rear ends floated.

DINOSAUR MARSHMALLOW MODEL

Think you can build a perfectly balanced dinosaur?
Try it out with this engineering challenge!

You Need

- Dinosaur toys or pictures (*T. rex* and *Brontosaurus*)
- Scissors
- Paper straws
- Large marshmallows
- Small marshmallows

1. Look at a picture or toy of a *T. rex*. Notice that it walks on two feet.

2. Brainstorm ideas for building a model of a *T. rex* out of marshmallows and straws. (You can cut the straws with the scissors to make them smaller.) Your dinosaur must have a body, a head, a tail, arms, and legs. And it must be able to stand up on its own.

3. Make a plan and build your model.

4. Once you succeed, look at the picture or toy of a *Brontosaurus*. Notice that it walks on four feet.

5. Brainstorm ideas about how you can transform your model to represent this kind of dinosaur. You can use additional straws and marshmallows.

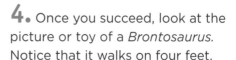

6. Make a plan and build your model. It must have a body, a head, a tail, and legs, and it must be able to stand up on its own.

How It Works:
The force of gravity pulls things toward the center of Earth. The center of gravity is the point where a body is in balance. If a body (or a dinosaur!) is not in balance, gravity will cause it to fall over. ∎

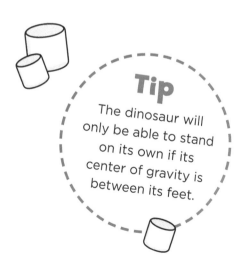

Tip
The dinosaur will only be able to stand on its own if its center of gravity is between its feet.

THE GREAT
OUTDOORS

Make a necklace or crown out of flowers. What kinds of flowers did you use?

Quick Challenges

Have a nature scavenger hunt. Try to find a white rock, a leaf with five points, a worm, and a yellow flower. Make a list of other things to find.

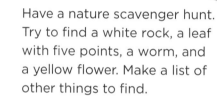

Search your community for animal tracks. Identify the tracks and create an animal track chart. Which animals visit the area most often?

Collect rocks and stack them into a tall tower. (Make sure you're allowed to take the rocks first!) Hint: Flatter rocks are easier to stack, and it pays to be patient!

With an adult, go for a hike. Take binoculars and a magnifying glass to see nature up close.

Build a sandcastle, a snow castle, or a fantastic structure out of mud. Glam up your building using natural materials like shells, leaves, and sticks.

How Do Plants Drink Water?

JUST LIKE YOU, PLANTS NEED water to live. But unlike you, they don't actually drink it.

Plants absorb water through a part called the *root*. A plant's roots are usually underground and help to hold the plant upright. They also get water and nutrients from the soil. Roots are covered in a very thin layer of cells called the *epidermis*. The epidermis has a selective barrier known as a *membrane* that keeps harmful things out of the roots but lets good things in, such as water. When a plant takes water into its roots through the membrane, it's called *osmosis*.

Once a plant has absorbed water into its roots, it moves the water up through its stem and to its leaves through a process called *capillary action*. Just as you have a system of blood vessels that carries nutrients through your body, plants also have a system of tubes. These tubes are called *xylem* and *phloem*. The xylem and phloem carry water, food, and minerals throughout the plant.

Water is very important to plants. They use water to help keep their shape and stay firm. They also use water to help turn sunlight into energy, sort of the way you eat food to make energy. So do like a plant does and stay hydrated!

HOW WATER MOVES THROUGH A PLANT

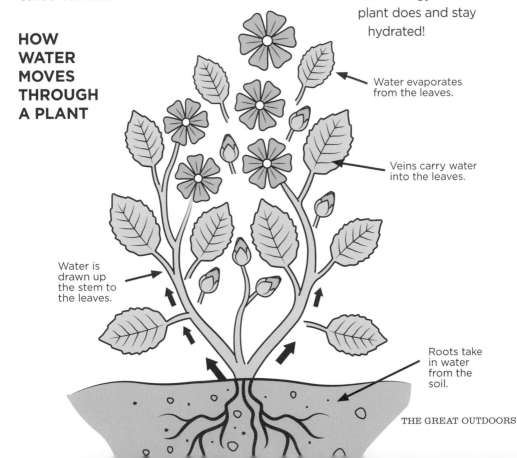

Water evaporates from the leaves.

Veins carry water into the leaves.

Water is drawn up the stem to the leaves.

Roots take in water from the soil.

CHANGE A FLOWER'S COLOR

With this experiment, you'll use food coloring to observe how a flower takes in water.

Tip

Any white flower will do, but carnations work very well for this experiment. Have an adult hold the stems underwater while cutting. This ensures no air bubbles get into the tubes, blocking the flow of water.

You Need

- 5 clear glasses or mason jars
- Food coloring
- White flowers
- Scissors

1. Fill each glass halfway with water. Set one glass aside.

2. Squirt a different color of food coloring into each of the four remaining glasses. Stir. Add more food coloring until the water is brightly colored.

3. Remove the leaves from the flowers.

4. Use scissors to trim about four inches off the bottom of each stem. Then cut the bottom of each stem at an angle.

5. Place one flower in each of the glasses, including the glass with clear water.

6. Let the flowers soak for several days. Watch to see what happens.

How It Works:

This experiment uses colorful water to show how the liquid travels through a plant. Water moves through tiny tubes in a flower's stem and petals through the process of *capillary action*—a liquid's ability to travel upward, against gravity, in narrow spaces. Then, water that has been pulled into the petals evaporates. The colorful water in this experiment leaves behind dye after evaporating. Once this water has left the plant, more water from the stem is pulled into the petals, adding additional color to them.

More Ideas

Have an adult split the flower stems halfway up with scissors. Place each split end in a glass filled with a different color.

WANDERING COLORS

Water moves through plants by "climbing up" tubes inside of them. Watch water climb paper towels with your own eyes.

Tip

Use a brand of paper towel that holds water well. Otherwise, your water will have trouble "walking" from one glass to the other.

★☆☆
Easy

You Need

- 6 paper towels (half-sheets)
- 6 wide-mouth glasses (or jars)
- Scissors (optional)
- Red, yellow, and blue food coloring

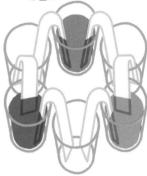

1. Fold each paper towel lengthwise into thirds, creating thin strips.

2. Place two glasses side by side. One at a time, check to make sure the paper towel strips are the right size. To do this, place one end of each strip in one glass, and the other end in the second glass. The arc at the top of each strip should rise just above the top of the glasses. Trim the ends of the strips if the arcs are too high. Then remove the paper towel strips from the glasses.

3. Line the glasses up.

4. Add a squirt of red food coloring to the first glass, yellow to the third glass, and blue to the fifth glass. Do not add any food coloring to the other glasses.

5. Fill each glass that contains food coloring to the top with water. Do not put any water in the other glasses.

6. Arrange the glasses into a circle in the following order: red, empty, yellow, empty, blue, empty.

7. Add the paper towel strips to the glasses, beginning with the red glass. Place one end of a strip in one glass and the other end in the glass next to it. Move around the circle until you've filled all the glasses with the paper towel strips.

8. Watch as the colored water "walks" from one glass to another, creating a beautiful rainbow.

How It Works:

In this experiment, water traveled up through the paper towels. (That's capillary action!) The color in the water helps you see how the water moved. In plants, capillary action helps water climb up from the roots all the way to the highest leaves. ■

How Do Mountains Form?

YOU PROBABLY CAN'T TELL, but the land you are on is always moving. The part of Earth you live on—the planet's outer shell—is called the crust. The crust is broken up into large pieces known as plates.

Beneath this outer crust, Earth is made up of different layers of hot, partially molten rock. Because these inner layers are so hot and flexible, the plates of the crust are always moving. They move so slowly that the movement is almost always unnoticeable to humans. This process is called *plate tectonics.*

However, even though it is slow, the movement is very powerful and can cause mountains to form. This often happens when different plates crash into each other. The pressure from the smashing plates causes part of the crust to thrust upward into the air, slowly forming a mountain or mountain range over many years.

Sometimes, one plate will force the other one beneath it in a process called *subduction*. The plate on top lifts up, also forming mountains. Other times, pressure in the crust can cause the earth to crack or buckle. This can send large chunks of earth upward or downward. It just goes to show that small actions and movements can lead to huge results!

How Do Earthquakes Happen?

EVEN THOUGH PLATE TECTONICS is a super slow process, it can still have huge impacts. Not only can the movements of Earth's plates create mountains (see page 128), it can also cause earthquakes.

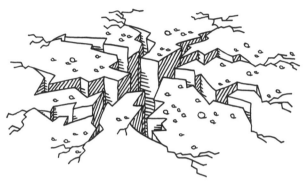

The outer layer of the planet, the crust, is broken up into different parts, called *plates*. These plates are always moving, thanks to the heat and flexibility of Earth's layers below. As the plates move, they crash together, slip over each other, pull apart, and slide alongside each other.

EARTHQUAKE SAFETY

If you are ever in an earthquake, remember these tips from earthquake safety experts.
1. Stay where you are. (If you are inside, stay inside, and if you are outside, stay outside.)
2. Drop to the ground on your hands and knees. Being close to the ground stops you from falling, but being on your hands and knees lets you continue to move if needed.
3. Cover as much of yourself as you're able—and especially your head and neck—under a sturdy table or desk. If there aren't any nearby, get next to a wall or low, stable furniture and cover your head and neck with your arms.
4. Hold on to your shelter or to yourself until the shaking stops.

Most of the time, you can't feel the plates moving. However, plates can come into contact in places known as *plate boundaries*. And sometimes they can get stuck. When the plates grind up against each other, it causes resistance—or *friction*. When the plates get stuck due to friction, pressure starts to build until there is enough force for the plates to come unstuck and keep moving. This force causes a ripple of energy that makes the ground shake—an earthquake.

During an earthquake, the ground can shake, roll, and buckle. Most earthquakes are so small that you can't feel them—in fact, earthquakes are happening all the time. But other earthquakes can be so powerful that they can destroy buildings and even cause giant waves known as *tsunamis*. Luckily, scientists have technology that lets them monitor *tremors*—small movements in the ground. This lets the scientists figure out where earthquakes may happen and prepare for them.

Easy

EDIBLE TECTONIC PLATES

Tectonic plates fit together like a giant jigsaw puzzle. An edge where two plates meet is called a plate boundary. There are three main types of tectonic plate boundaries: divergent, transform, and convergent. In this sweet experiment, you'll use graham crackers to re-create all three!

Divergent

You Need

- Table knife
- 3 paper plates
- Whipped cream, peanut butter, or frosting
- Graham crackers
- Water

Transform

Convergent

1. Cover each paper plate with a half-inch-thick layer of whipped cream, peanut butter, or frosting. This substance represents *magma* (molten rock) in the *mantle*, the layer just beneath the crust on Earth's surface. Use the knife to cover each.

2. Break each graham cracker in half horizontally along the perforation in the middle. Lay the pieces of graham cracker next to each other on each plate, smooth sides touching. The graham crackers represent tectonic plates.

3. Create a divergent boundary on the first plate. Gently press down on the graham crackers as you pull them away from each other. What happens to the mantle in the middle?

4. Create a transform boundary on the second plate. Keep the graham crackers together. With their sides touching, slowly slide one cracker up as you slide the other cracker down. How does it feel when the tectonic plates slide against each other?

5. Create a convergent boundary on the third plate. Dip the long edge of one graham cracker in water. Put the cracker back on the plate with the soggy edge facing the other graham cracker. Gently push the two graham crackers together. Can you see the "mountains" form?

GELATIN EARTHQUAKE

Build an earthquake-proof building out of marshmallows and toothpicks.

Tip
Shorter buildings are more stable than taller buildings. Triangles add strength to the base.

You Need

- Packet of gelatin
- Water
- Cookie sheet
- Toothpicks
- Mini marshmallows
- Scissors
- Stopwatch

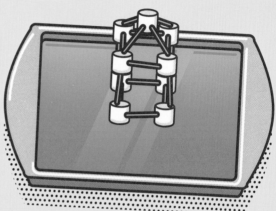

1. With an adult's help, prepare the gelatin by following the instructions on the package. Pour the gelatin onto the cookie sheet. Refrigerate it until it is firm.

2. Use the toothpicks and mini marshmallows to build five structures of different shapes and sizes. You can cut the toothpicks with scissors if you'd like to use smaller pieces. But you must use the same number of toothpicks and marshmallows in each structure.

3. Examine your finished structures. Predict which structures will stand the longest during an earthquake.

4. Put your predictions to the test. Place the first structure on the sheet of gelatin. Shake the cookie back and forth. Keep time to see how long it takes for the structure to fall.

5. Repeat with the other structures. Be sure to shake equally hard on each try.

More Ideas

- Try testing multiple structures at once. The strongest structure is the last one standing.
- Chill the gelatin in a smaller, deeper pan, like an 8-by-8-inch baking dish. It will shake more, creating a more volatile earthquake.

BUILD A SEISMOGRAPH

A *seismograph* is an instrument that detects earthquakes and measures how powerful they are. See how a seismograph measures movement during an earthquake.

You Need

- Medium cardboard box
- Scissors
- Paper cup
- String
- Tape
- Marker
- Coins, marbles, or other small, heavy objects to use as weights
- 1 or more long, printed store receipts

FOR TWO SCIENTISTS

1. Cut the top flaps off the cardboard box. Stand the box up on one of its shorter sides. Cut slits near the bottom edge on each side of the box. The slits must be directly across from each other and wide enough for the receipt to pass through.

2. Under the rim of the cup, use scissors to poke two small holes across from each other.

3. Cut a hole in the center of the bottom of the cup. This hole should be large enough for a marker to poke through.

4. Poke two holes in the middle of the top of the box. The distance between these holes should equal the distance between the holes under the rim of the cup.

5. Cut two pieces of string, each slightly longer than the long side of the box.

6. Thread a string through one hole in the cup. Tie it. Repeat with the other string on the opposite side of the cup.

7. Push the other end of each string through the holes in the top of the box. Adjust the strings until 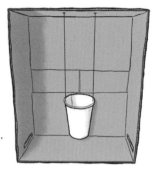 the cup is level and the bottom of the cup is about an inch above the bottom of the box. Tie the strings together and tape them in place.

8. Remove the cap from the marker. Push the marker through the hole until its tip barely touches  the bottom of the box. Fill the cup with small, heavy objects. If necessary, use tape to keep the marker vertical and hold it in place.

9. Tape the receipts together to make one long strip. Thread the strip through the slits in the bottom of the box. Make sure the marker is centered on the strip.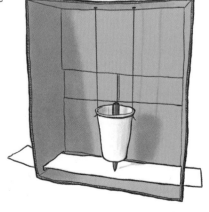

10. Have Partner 1 hold the box, gently shake it—keeping the bottom of the box on the table—pause, and repeat.

11. As this occurs, have Partner 2 slowly pull the strip through the slits at the bottom of the box. Partner 2 should try to maintain a steady speed.

12. When you reach the end of the strip, examine the results.

How It Works:
The jagged line on the receipt tells you how hard the box was shaken. Larger curves in the line mean harder shakes. Smaller curves mean gentler shakes. Real seismographs have a similar way of showing the strength of an earthquake. ■

THE GREAT OUTDOORS | **133**

How Do Volcanoes Erupt?

OUR PLANET IS MOSTLY MADE up of hot, shifting rock. The part you live on, the *crust*, is broken into pieces called *plates* that sit on the shifting rock and slowly move around.

Sometimes, two plates run into each other and one plate slides beneath the other. This process is called *subduction*. During subduction, the plate that has been pushed below the surface causes the crust above to buckle, forming mountains. Sometimes, the plate underneath even melts, leading molten rock to bubble up to the surface and form volcanoes. This can happen on land or deep underneath the ocean.

Other volcanoes form mostly underwater in a process called *diversion*, when two plate boundaries pull away from each other. As they separate, hot magma oozes up from inside the earth. Some of the magma builds up and cools, forming chains of volcanoes all around the globe.

Occasionally, volcanoes can even form over places where superhot magma melts away Earth's crust and builds up. These places are called *hot spots*.

Just as volcanoes form in different ways, they also erupt in different ways. When magma continues to build in volcanoes, it slowly fills the chambers deep inside. Over time, it can overflow through vents and cracks. But sometimes, the magma can get trapped or can be too thick to flow out. In these cases, gases build up inside the volcano. If the gases can't get out, pressure begins to grow. Once the pressure is too great—*boom!*—the volcano erupts, spewing lava and ash.
.

ABOUT TO BLOW!

Scientists can keep people who live near volcanoes safe by looking out for signs of volcanic activity. One of the ways they do this is by studying earthquakes in the area. Increases in magma and gases can make pressure build up, causing small earthquakes known as *tremors*. When there are more tremors than usual, it might mean that a volcano will soon erupt.

Ash →

Erupting Lava →

Vent →

MAKE AN APPLE ERUPTION

Lava may not ooze from its core, but an apple volcano is a great way to explore chemistry in your kitchen!

Tip

To avoid wasting good food, try to use an apple that's about to go bad.

You Need

- Apple
- Knife
- Dish with sides
- Baking soda
- Dish soap
- Food coloring
- Dropper
- Vinegar

1. Have an adult cut out the middle of the apple. Don't go all the way through to the bottom (the apple should be able to hold water).

2. Put the apple on the dish.

3. Fill the middle of the apple about three-quarters full with baking soda.

4. Add several drops of dish soap and a few drops of food coloring.

5. Fill the dropper with vinegar. Slowly squirt the vinegar into the apple.

6. Watch the apple erupt!

How It Works:

Vinegar is an acid. Baking soda is a base. When the two combine, a chemical reaction occurs. The dish soap and food coloring just make the reaction bubblier and more colorful.

More Ideas

Try this experiment with a lemon. Cut the lemon in half. Put half of the lemon on a plate. Poke the top of the lemon with a fork. Add food coloring and dish soap. Watch the "volcano" begin to erupt once you add baking soda to the fruit. (There's no need for vinegar. The acid is already inside the lemon.)

CREATE AN UNDERWATER VOLCANO

Lava is hot. Add a bit of cold and you can create a cool underwater eruption.

Tip
Try the experiment using warm water, not hot. Compare the results.

You Need

- Large, tall clear container
- Small clear container (that fits inside the larger one)
- Small rocks or coins
- Water
- Food coloring
- Skewer or small wooden spoon

1. Fill the large container with very cold water.

2. Put several small rocks or coins in the small container to make it heavier.

3. With an adult's help, fill the small container with very hot water. Add a few drops of food coloring. Stir with a skewer or small wooden spoon.

4. Have the adult hold the small container upright and gently release it into the large container.

5. Watch the colored water erupt like a volcano!

How It Works:

Hot water is less dense than cold water. When you drop the hot, colored water into the container of cold water, the hot water rises to the top. The cold water sinks to the bottom. As the hot and cold water mix and all of the water becomes warm, the color spreads evenly throughout the container. ■

Safety Tip

The small container may feel hot when filled with very hot water. To prevent burns, have the adult helping you wear oven mitts or hold the container with a towel.

How Do Flowers Get Their Scents?

FROM ROSES TO JASMINE TO LILIES, many flowers smell wonderful. Others don't seem to have any smell at all. And there are even flowers that stink!

As much as we might love the scent of certain flowers, the plants don't make their smells for us. Scented flowers smell the way they do to attract insects and other pollinating animals. Lots of flowers do this in order to *reproduce*, or create new flowers.

Flowering plants reproduce through a process called *pollination*. To create a seed, two different flower parts need to interact: a cluster of tiny grains known as *pollen* and a specialized flower part called the *stigma*. Some flowers have both of these parts and can create seeds on their own. Other flowers rely on the wind to blow their pollen to another plant's stigma. These flowers often don't have any scent.

However, other flowers rely on animals—like bats, bees, flies, beetles, and butterflies—to carry pollen from one flower to another.

To attract these pollinators, flowers create different scents that the animals will find appealing. Depending on the animal, their favorite scent could be sweet-smelling or stinky.

Some flowers create these aromas by producing oily chemicals in their petals. When these oils *evaporate*—or turn into gases—they can travel far and wide through the air. Other flowers, like orchids, have special organs just for making scents. Some flowers even send out their scents during certain times of day or night to attract specific animals. Makes scents!

STINKY FLOWERS

Some types of flowers, such as the carrion flower, need to attract insects that don't necessarily love sweet smells. In fact, some of these insects, like flies, are attracted to the smell of rotting meat! The carrion flower takes advantage of this by mimicking the stench to lure flies. When the fly zips between multiple smelly carrion flowers, it will pick up pollen and help carry it to other flowers, helping to pollinate the plants.

★★★
Hard

MAKE ROSE POTPOURRI

Capture the sweet scent of flowers in a jar! With dried flower petals and a few other ingredients, you can create a naturally fragrant concoction called potpourri.

You Need

- 6 cups rose petals
- Cookie sheet (optional)
- 3 cinnamon sticks
- Few drops of essential oil
- 1 glass jar with lid
- Decorative dish

1. Lay the rose petals on a flat surface. Let them dry for several days. Or, with an adult's help, dehydrate the rose petals in the oven: Spread the petals on a cookie sheet and bake at 180°F for 15–30 minutes.

2. Combine the petals, cinnamon sticks, and drops of essential oil in the jar. Screw on the lid.

3. Let the jar sit, shaking it every other day, for at least a week.

4. Display your finished potpourri in a decorative dish.

More Ideas

Sew two small pieces of fabric together to make a pillow. Fill the pillow with potpourri before sewing it shut.

KEEP FLOWERS SMELLING FRESH

Use science to keep cut flowers looking and smelling great for a little bit longer.

You Need

- Index cards
- Marker
- 10 tall thin glasses
- Water
- 1 teaspoon measuring spoon
- Sugar
- Vinegar
- Bleach
- 10 identical flowers
- Scissors
- Refrigerator

1. Label the index cards as follows: *water/cut; water/uncut; sugar/cut; sugar/uncut; vinegar/cut; vinegar/uncut; bleach/cut; bleach/uncut; refrigerator/cut; refrigerator/uncut.*

2. Lay the index cards out on a table. Place a glass on each card. Fill each glass two-thirds full of water.

3. Add two teaspoons of sugar to each "sugar" glass. Stir.

4. Add two teaspoons of vinegar to each "vinegar" glass. Stir.

5. Have an adult help you add two teaspoons of bleach to each "bleach" glass. Stir.

6. Using scissors, cut the bottom of five flowers at a slant. Do not cut the other flowers.

7. Place a flower in each glass. Make sure to put the cut flowers in the glasses labeled with cut and the uncut flowers labeled with uncut.

8. Place all glasses containing flowers in water, sugar, vinegar, and bleach in a sunny spot. Put the two flowers in "refrigerator" glasses in the refrigerator.

9. Observe and smell the flowers every day for a week. Change the water—and add the appropriate ingredients—on day three. Which conditions kept your flowers looking great and smelling fresh the longest? ■

Safety Tip

Bleach can burn your skin. Ask for an adult's help when handling the bleach. If you do get bleach on your skin, wash your hands thoroughly with soap and water.

How Do Icicles Become Pointy?

IF YOU TAKE A LOOK AT THE branches of trees or the roof of a house during a sunny winter's day, you might see icicles forming. These thin cones of frozen water need just the right conditions to form.

First, there must be lots of water present, usually in the form of snow. Next, there needs to be sunlight to start melting the snow. Finally, temperatures must be below freezing—otherwise the sun will melt the snow into liquid form without it freezing back into ice.

If all these conditions are met, the snow along the sides of a roof, on top of branches, or along other edges where it has collected may start to melt under the sunlight. But because it's freezing out, the melted water that drips off the edge will start to freeze again.

At first, the frozen water will form clumps of ice along the edge it's dripping from. But as more water melts and runs down the ice, pointy icicles will start to form. This is due to two things: gravity and heat loss.

Thanks to gravity, water drips downward. But as it travels farther away from the base of the icicle, it loses heat. The drop becomes colder and colder, until it finally freezes again at the icicle's tip—forming a point.

SNOW WHITE

Snow—clean snow, at least—looks like it is pure white. Why is that? This is because of the way snow crystals reflect light. When light hits snow, the crystals reflect back every color. To the human eye, the combination of all these colors appears white.

MAKE RAINBOW ICICLES

You can do science in all kinds of weather! Follow these instructions when the temperature drops below freezing (32°F) to create amazing colorful icicles.

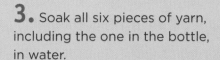

Tip

In step 9, use cold water. If you use hot water, you will melt the icicles that have already formed.

You Need

- Yarn or string
- Scissors
- 2-liter plastic bottle
- Water
- Ladder
- Broomstick
- 5 medium-sized rocks or weights
- Cookie sheet or tray
- Pitcher
- Food coloring

3. Soak all six pieces of yarn, including the one in the bottle, in water.

4. As the yarn soaks, go outside. With the help of an adult, set up a ladder. Slide the broomstick across the middle steps.

5. Bring your bottle and wet yarn outside. Have an adult place the bottle on the top step of the ladder. (DO NOT climb up the ladder at any point.) Tie the yarn dangling from the bottle to the broomstick.

1. Cut six long pieces of yarn or string.

2. Make a small hole in the bottom of the 2-liter bottle. Thread one piece of yarn through the hole.

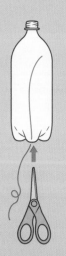

6. Tie the other five pieces of wet yarn to the broomstick. Check to make sure that all six pieces of yarn are touching at the spot where they're tied on the broomstick.

7. Branch out the five lower pieces of yarn from the broomstick like a tent. Tie each piece of yarn around a rock. Set the rocks or weights on the cookie sheet or tray and place under the ladder.

9. Repeat step 8 every 10 minutes for an hour or two. Add different colors of food coloring to the water each time.

10. Let the icicles freeze overnight. Then check out the layers of color in your rainbow icicles! ■

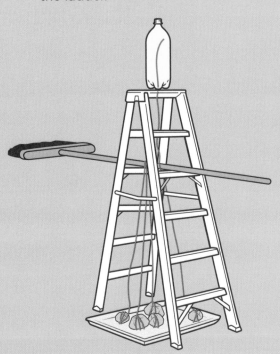

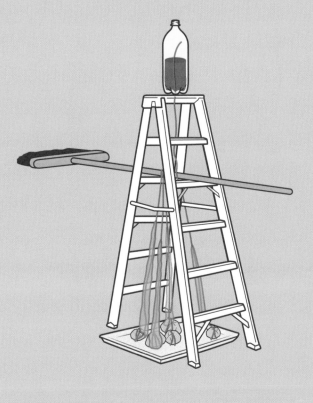

8. Inside, fill a pitcher with cold water. Stir in a few drops of food coloring. With help from an adult, carefully pour the water from the pitcher into the 2-liter bottle on the ladder. Let the water drip down the yarn.

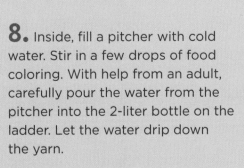

How Do Deserts Get Sand?

WHEN YOU PICTURE A DESERT, you might imagine rolling dunes of golden sand. But not all deserts are sandy! In fact, Antarctica is a desert. A desert is a dry place that gets very little rain or snow.

In Antarctica, much of the ground is covered with ice or rock. In other deserts, such as in the southwestern United States, the ground is hard and dry, like cracked clay. And some deserts, like the Sahara in Africa, are covered in hills of sand.

Deserts form over thousands—or even millions—of years, thanks to shifting weather patterns around the world. In some places, like polar deserts, freezing temperatures keep the large ice sheets intact even though there is no rain or snow. The ice also helps reflect heat back toward space. But in most deserts, lack of rain and a dry, hot sun means that there is no moisture for plants. Over time, all moisture dries up from the earth, causing plants to largely disappear. The ground becomes bare and dry.

In some of these places, a process called *erosion* begins to happen. Erosion is when rocks or minerals begin to break apart and break down into tiny particles—sand. Sand can come from erosion in nearby mountains, or from the ground itself once it has dried up. As soil becomes drier and drier, it often turns from solid earth into loose dirt, dust, and sand over many, many years. Winds can sweep away much of the dirt and dust, leaving the sand.

In places like the Sahara, winds can also tumble this sand over onto itself, driving it into those picturesque dunes.

LIFE IN THE DESERT

Deserts are very dry places with little water and almost no plants. But across the world, animals have adapted to survive in these landscapes. Some animals, like the sand cats of northern Africa and western Asia, get water from the food they eat. Others, including small mammals like the kangaroo rats found in North America, burrow underground to stay cool. And still others have furry paws that help them run across shifting sands—like the fennec foxes of northern Africa.

Fennec Fox

CLOSE-UP ON SAND

There are different kinds of sand, and each
has its own special characteristics.

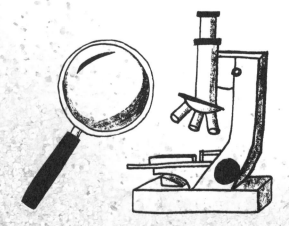

You Need

- Plastic wrap
- Different kinds of sand
- Spoons
- White paper
- Magnifying glass
- Black paper
- Microscope (optional)

1. Tear off several small pieces of
plastic wrap.

2. Scoop a small amount of each
type of sand into a separate piece of
plastic wrap. Use a separate spoon
for each type of sand so you don't
mix the samples.

3. Rub each type of sand through
your fingers. Notice that different
kinds of sand have different textures.

4. Lay the pieces of plastic wrap
with the sand samples on the white
paper.

5. Examine each type of sand with
the magnifying glass. Observe the
size, shape, color, and texture of the
particles.

6. Lay the pieces of plastic wrap
with the sand samples on the black
paper. Observe again. It may be
easier to examine certain colors
of sand on the darker paper.

7. If you have access to a
microscope, use it to examine each
type of sand. How do the sand
particles look different when you
see them closer up? ■

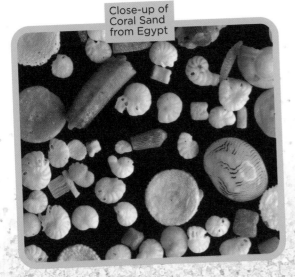

Close-up of Coral Sand from Egypt

Close-up of Sand from Coral Pink Sand Dunes State Park, Utah

Close-up of White Beach Sand from the Mediterranean

Close-up of Volcanic Sand from Iran

Close-up of Star-Shaped Sand from Okinawa, Japan

Did You Know?

The characteristics of sand depend on what the sand is made of and the environmental conditions present when it was formed.

How Do Tree Leaves Change Color?

WINTER IS OFTEN FUN AND beautiful. It can also be a time for lots of living things to eat delicious food, hunker down in a cozy spot, and get some rest. Trees are no exception!

Most trees have leaves that are normally green. This is because the leaves are full of a chemical called *chlorophyll*. Chlorophyll helps plants turn sunlight into energy in a process called *photosynthesis*. During photosynthesis, chlorophyll absorbs energy from sunlight and uses this energy to create nutrients. Because plants depend on chlorophyll for nutrients, they need a lot of it. And chlorophyll happens to appear green!

But during the winter, temperatures can drop below freezing. This freezes the trees' leaves, and the chlorophyll inside them, too. So when it starts to get colder in the fall, rather than lose the valuable chlorophyll completely, the trees break it down and store its nutrients for later use someplace safe—in their roots. The roots stay warmer underground, where they are protected from the elements. This makes them a good storage place for energy and nutrients.

As the chlorophyll breaks down, the green color starts to disappear from the leaves. However, there are still other compounds, called *pigments*, left in the leaves. These pigments can turn the leaves into those beautiful shades of red, yellow, and orange that the fall season is so famous for.

Chlorophyll breaking down and leaving a leaf is one of the first steps of the leaf beginning to die. After the tree has taken back all the nutrients it can, the dying leaves begin to fall, eventually turning brown and crispy. This process protects the health of the tree and makes room for new leaves next spring.

COLOR–CHANGING CREATURES

Leaves aren't the only things that change color in winter. Lots of animals do, too! Many animals that live in cold places—such as Arctic hares, certain weasels, Arctic foxes, and more—grow thick white winter coats. Not only does the extra fur keep them warm, the white helps camouflage them against the snow.

Arctic Fox

LEAF CHROMATOGRAPHY

Discover what gives leaves their amazing fall colors!

You Need

- Leaves of different colors
- Scissors
- Glass jars
- Wooden spoons
- Rubbing alcohol
- Paper towels
- Ruler

Tip

Place the glasses in a baking dish. With an adult's help, fill the dish with boiling water. (Don't put the water in the glasses!) This will warm the alcohol and speed up the experiment.

1. In the fall, go outside and collect fallen leaves. Sort the leaves by color (red, yellow, green, etc.) Try to get about 10 leaves for each color. The brighter the colors in the leaves are, the better this experiment will work.

2. Cut the stems off one color of leaves. Cut the leaves into tiny pieces. Put the pieces of leaf in a glass jar. Label the glass so you know which color of leaf it contains.

3. Crush the leaves with the end of the wooden spoon until the leaves release their juices. Then pour rubbing alcohol into the jar so the leaves are covered. Crush the leaves with the wooden spoon some more.

4. Repeat steps 2 and 3 with the leaves of other colors. Use a separate jar for each color. If you only have one wooden spoon, wash it before using it on a different color.

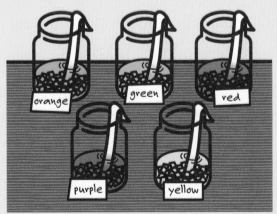

orange   green   red

purple   yellow

5. Cut paper towels into one-inch-wide strips. Place one strip in each glass, draping it over the side of the glass. Let the glasses sit overnight.

6. Remove the strips. Let the strips dry. Observe the bands of colors.

How It Works:
Leaves contain different *pigments*, or substances that give things color. When combined with alcohol, the colors in a leaf travel up the paper towel at different speeds. This causes the colors to separate. The process of separating the parts of a mixture—like the colors of a leaf—is called *chromatography.* ■

WILD
WEATHER

Quick Challenges

Create shadow drawings! Place a small toy on a piece of drawing paper in the sun. Trace its shadow. Leave the toy there and come back later in the day to trace its shadow again.

Look for shapes in the clouds. Recognize anything? Recreate the shapes with cotton balls.

Have an ice cube race. Put one ice cube on a dark piece of paper and one on a white piece. Put them both in the sun. Which cube melts faster?

Make fog! Put your face close to a cool window or mirror. Open your mouth wide and breathe on the glass.

Place a paper cup outside the next time it rains. After the rain stops, use a ruler to measure how much rain fell.

Design a vehicle that would have no problem going through a downpour, hailstorm, or blizzard.

How Do Clouds Get Their Shapes?

THE CLOUDS ABOVE YOU MIGHT look puffy enough to hug, but they're actually made of water.

Water can take three forms: It can be a liquid, like when it's in the ocean; a solid, like when it's frozen into ice; and an invisible gas in the air called *water vapor*. When liquid water meets warm air, it often turns into water vapor in a process called *evaporation*. This warm air and water vapor rise into the sky, where it is colder. There, the vapor

starts to cool back down. Cold air can't hold vapor like warm air can, so the cool water comes back together in a process called *condensation*, forming lots of tiny droplets of water.

Clouds are made of these tiny droplets of water. Even though these clouds can look like thick cotton, they are actually light and wispy. Because of this, the air flowing around them can easily mold them into the different shapes you see.

BECOME A METEOROLOGIST

Study the weather, and then use what you've observed to predict future weather conditions.

You Need

- Piece of paper or notebook
- Pen or pencil
- Markers or colored pencils
- Outdoor thermometer

1. Choose a time of day to go outside. Bring a piece of paper or a notebook with you. This is your weather journal.

2. Record the amount of sun and clouds and any precipitation you observe using words and pictures.

3. Record the temperature using the thermometer.

4. Repeat steps 1, 2, and 3 for three days. Try to go outside at the same time every day.

5. After the third day, read through your journal. Did you notice any patterns in the weather? Can you guess what the weather will be the following day? Write down your prediction in your weather journal. Were you right?

CLOUD TYPES

Fluffy, puffy, feathery—clouds come in many different forms. Sometimes we can tell what the weather might be just by observing what the clouds look like. Here are three common types of clouds you might see:

- **Cirrus clouds** are white, thin, and wispy. Usually the weather is fair and sunny when there are cirrus clouds—but they also can mean the weather is about to change.
- **Stratus clouds** can cover the sky like a gray blanket. This type of cloud often means it's going to rain or snow.
- **Cumulonimbus clouds** are storm clouds. They're tall, dark, and can mean lightning and thunder are on the way.

CLOUD IN A JAR

You may have everything you need at home to make a cloud right in your kitchen.

Tip
If the bottle gets foggy before you spray the hair spray, swish the water around the bottle gently to clear the fog away.

You Need

- Hot water
- Glass jar with metal lid
- Ice cubes
- Aerosol hair spray

1. Have an adult help you heat up some water. The water should be hot but not boiling. Warm up the jar by filling it about one-third full with the hot water. Gently swirl the water so it warms the sides of the jar, too. Leave the water in the jar.

2. Set the lid upside down on top of the jar. Put as many ice cubes as will fit on top of the lid. Wait about 20 seconds.

3. Slide the lid with the ice still on it out of the way so you can quickly spray a little bit of hair spray into the jar. Replace the lid.

4. Watch your cloud form! What you see is what it looks like inside a cloud.

How It Works:
Clouds form when water vapor condenses, forming little droplets around tiny bits of dust, sea salt, or other particles in the sky. In this activity, water vapor condenses around little bits of hair spray. ∎

How Does Lightning Happen?

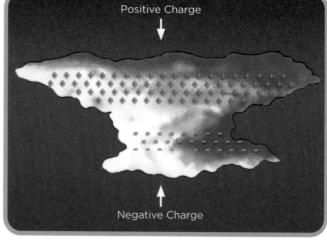

Positive Charge

Negative Charge

CRACK! **WHETHER YOU** think lightning is scary, awesome, or somewhere in between, there's no denying that it is an incredible force of nature.

Lightning gets its start in something very small: the tiny water droplets that make up clouds. When clouds are high in the sky, freezing temperatures can turn some of these tiny droplets into small ice crystals. When the ice and water droplets rub up against each other, they create static electricity—the same thing that can happen if you shuffle across a carpet in socks or rub a balloon.

In some clouds, all this bumping can create a negative electric charge at the bottom of the cloud, and a positive charge near the top of the cloud. These opposite charges attract one another—they pull on each other like magnets do.

The charges in the cloud continue to build up and pull on each other other until—*zap!*—a bolt of lightning jumps through the cloud. Most of the time, these powerful surges of lightning stay in the air and don't hit the earth.

But sometimes the negative charge at the bottom of the cloud is enough to attract positive charges on the ground below it. If enough energy builds, the two charges connect— *flash!*—there is a surge of electricity between the earth and the sky.

WHAT CAUSES THUNDER?

Because lightning is made up of an enormous surge of electricity, it is hot—very hot. In fact, the lightning is so sizzling hot that it causes the air around it to heat up in an instant. When this air heats, it expands super quickly and pushes outward, causing a shock wave. This shock wave causes the giant thunderclap you hear. Because light travels faster than sound does, you might see the lightning before you hear it!

LIGHT IT UP

You might be shocked to find you can easily make your own lightning bolt at home!

You Need

- 12-by-12-inch piece of aluminum foil
- Large glass jar with metal lid (If there is a plastic liner on the inside of the lid, remove it.)
- Metal thumbtacks with no paint on their heads
- Dryer sheet
- Small balloon, inflated and tied

1. Fold the aluminum foil in half vertically once then horizontally once so that you have a smaller square. Put it in the bottom of the jar. (Make it as flat as you can, but it's okay if it's not perfectly flat.)

2. Push the thumbtacks through the middle of the dryer sheet. Place the dryer sheet over the mouth of the jar with the thumbtacks pointing down. Hold the dryer sheet so it stays stretched across the jar opening, and screw on the lid.

3. Rub the balloon on your head until your hair starts to stick to it.

4. Touch the balloon to the metal lid. Watch what happens. Do you see lightning?

How It Works:
Rubbing the balloon on your head causes a buildup of static electricity—a charge that's stuck in one place and doesn't go anywhere. This buildup occurs because the balloon pulls tiny particles called electrons away from your hair. They're stuck on the balloon until they touch the metal lid. Metal is a conductor—and electrons move through conductors extremely well. When the balloon touches the metal, the electrons move through the metal lid and thumbtacks. They jump through the air in the jar to the metal aluminum foil at the bottom of the jar, making a spark. ■

More Ideas

• See what happens if you rub the balloon on a wool sock or sweater instead of your hair.
• Try this experiment on a rainy day and on a clear, sunny day. Is there a difference?

How Do Animals Sense a Storm Coming?

WHEN HUMANS WANT TO FIGURE out if a storm is coming, we can check a few things (besides a weather app!). In addition to high-tech computers and satellites, humans are alerted to approaching storms by the shapes of the clouds, the color of the sky, or an increase in wind. For all these weather changes, people rely mostly on their senses of sight and touch—though some say they can also smell a difference in the air.

Thanks to the differences in many animals' senses, they have additional ways of telling if a storm might be approaching. Scientists think that some animals, such as birds and bees, can sense a change in the air pressure that sometimes indicates a storm is on its way. Ocean animals like sharks might also be able to sense this change of pressure in the water. Or, like some humans, animals such as cats and dogs can likely smell chemical changes in the air. Scientists think that animals with great hearing—such as elephants—may even be able to hear storms many miles away! With all these skills, it seems like animals have no need for weather apps.

UNDER PRESSURE

What is air pressure? Even though it may seem weightless, the air above us actually creates weight. Air pressure is the measurement of this weight. Air pressure is different in different parts of the world; for example, there is less air pressure high up in the mountains, and more air pressure at low-lying places like the sea. The heat from the sun also changes the air pressure in different places (see page 170). When there is high air pressure, the weather is usually calm. But low air pressure allows lots of changes to happen in the atmosphere, creating clouds, storms, and more. Scientists can study the weather by studying air pressure.

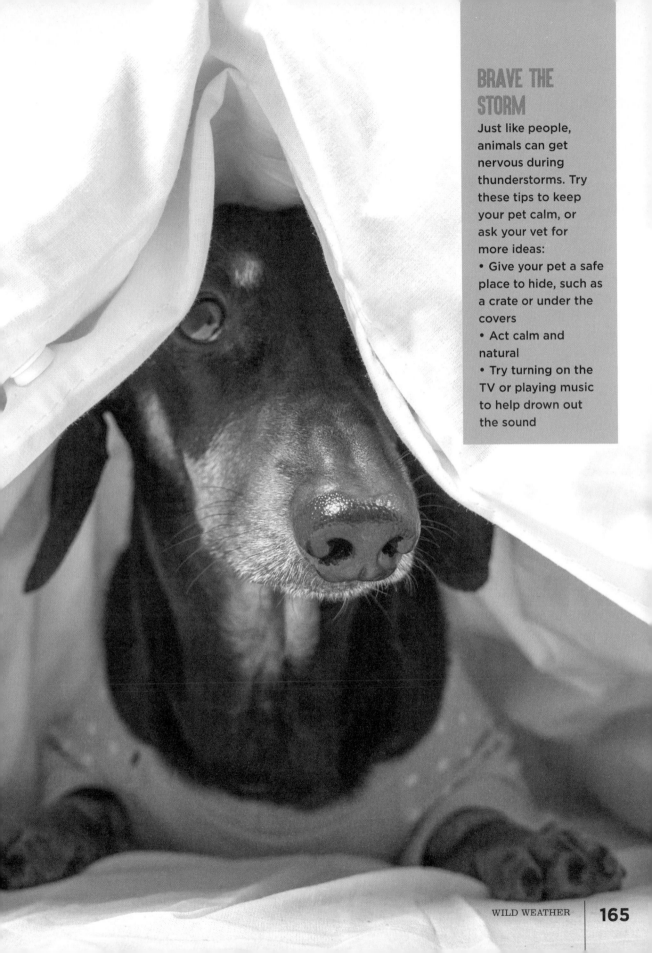

BRAVE THE STORM

Just like people, animals can get nervous during thunderstorms. Try these tips to keep your pet calm, or ask your vet for more ideas:
• Give your pet a safe place to hide, such as a crate or under the covers
• Act calm and natural
• Try turning on the TV or playing music to help drown out the sound

MAKE A BAROMETER

Some animals can sense changes in air pressure, which alerts them that a storm is coming. Meteorologists also use air pressure to predict the weather, employing tools called *barometers* to monitor the atmosphere for changes. Make your own barometer to predict the weather!

You Need

- Empty metal can with the top removed
- Petroleum jelly, such as Vaseline
- Balloon big enough to stretch over the can
- Scissors
- Rubber band
- Drinking straw (if you use a bendable straw, cut the flexible end off completely)
- Tape
- Light-colored heavy paper or poster board
- Pen or pencil

2. Cut the neck off the balloon. Stretch the uninflated balloon over the top edge of the can as tightly as possible, and then use the rubber band to hold it in place.

1. Carefully spread a small amount of petroleum jelly along the top edge of the can.

3. Lay one end of the straw in the middle of the balloon. Tape it in place.

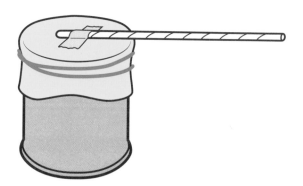

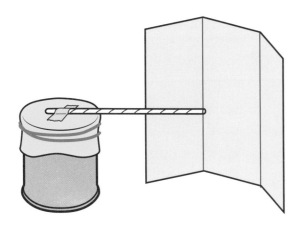

7. Make a note of what the weather is like when your barometer's straw changes.

How It Works:
The balloon is flexible, so it responds to air pressure. When air pressure is high, it pushes down on the balloon more. The straw tilts up. When air pressure is low, it pushes down on the balloon less. The straw tilts down.

4. Fold the paper or poster board into thirds lengthwise. Unfold it, then stand it next to the can. The tip of the straw should be right in front of the paper.

5. Use the pen or pencil to mark the spot where the tip of the straw sits in front of the paper. This is your barometer's first air pressure measurement.

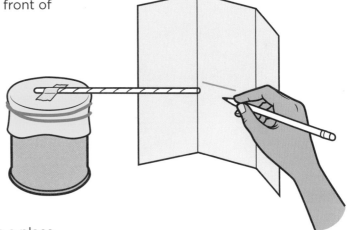

6. Place your barometer in a place where it won't be disturbed. Check your barometer a few times a day. If the tip of the straw moves, make another mark on the paper. Label the highest spot *high* and the lowest spot *low.*

ALTITUDE AND AIR PRESSURE

Air pressure has an effect on weather. It also helps explain why it is harder to breathe on the top of a mountain than at the bottom. Find out why with this model.

1. Ask an adult to help you poke three holes in the side of the carton opposite its opening: one near the bottom, one near the middle, and one near the top.

2. Place the carton in the sink with its opening under the faucet.

3. Turn on the faucet and fill the carton.

4. Compare how the water looks as it comes out of each hole.

How It Works:

Air pressure basically tells us the weight of the air above us. At the bottom of the atmosphere where we live, there's a lot of air above us, and the weight of all that air forces the air molecules to be close together. At the top of a mountain, there is less air weight above us, so the air is "thinner"—the particles that make up air, including oxygen molecules, are more spread out. That means that when we breathe at higher altitudes, we are taking in less oxygen with each breath. We need more breaths to get the same amount of oxygen we could get with fewer breaths at a lower altitude.

This model uses water to represent air. The water coming out of the bottom hole is under the most pressure. It has the weight of all of the water on top of it, so it is forced out of the carton the hardest. The water at the top of the carton doesn't have a lot of force pushing on it, so it trickles out of the hole. ■

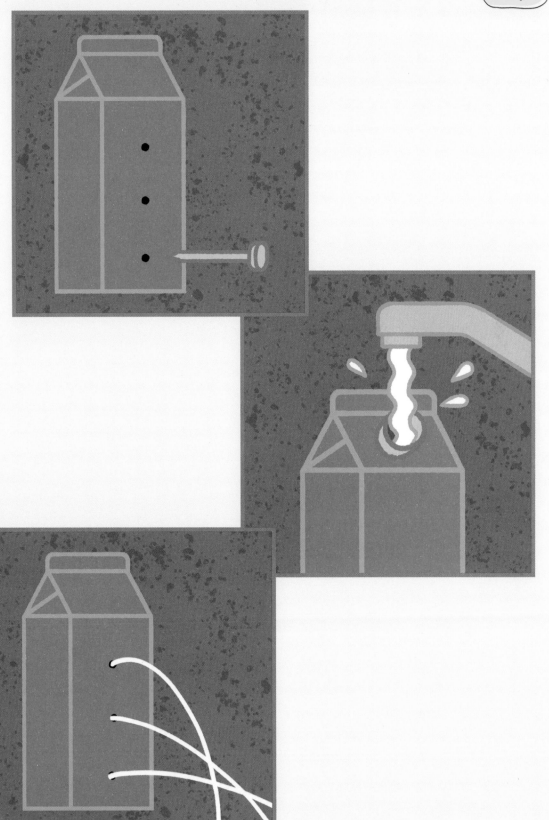

How Does the Wind Blow?

SOME DAYS IT'S WINDY; SOME DAYS it's perfectly still. Other days, the wind can blow hard enough to bend trees or even damage houses. All wind is caused by the same thing: the sun.

The sun is constantly putting out energy, known as *radiation*. This radiation travels through space to Earth, where it comes into contact with our atmosphere. There, the energy warms the atmosphere and the entire planet. But it doesn't warm the planet evenly; some parts receive more radiation than others.

The bits of air that are warmer tend to rise, which pulls in cooler air behind it. We know this moving air as wind. Earth's rotation causes our planet's wind patterns to shift in something called the Coriolis effect. The Coriolis effect can cause winds to twist in different directions; in the Northern Hemisphere winds twist to the right, and in the Southern Hemisphere they twist to the left.

Dust Devil
on Mars

OUT-OF-THIS-WORLD WIND

If wind is caused by the sun and the planet's rotation, is there wind on other planets? Yes! Just like Earth, most planets in our solar system have an atmosphere. This means that the sun's radiation causes wind on these planets, too. On Mars, wind can sometimes kick up the dusty soil to cause *dust devils*—small, swirling columns of air that are visible thanks to the dust and debris they've sucked up. As you get farther out into the solar system, the winds on different planets get more intense. Scientists think that might be because these planets' atmospheres offer less resistance to the wind to slow them down. In fact, winds on Neptune can travel more than 1,000 miles per hour—faster than the speed of sound on Earth!

WATERY WIND MODEL

Wind is an important part of our weather, whether it's a breeze, gust, or gale. Explore what makes the wind blow in this experiment by using water. (You'll want to do this activity in a sink or the tub.)

More Ideas

Empty the bottles and try the experiment again. What happens when you pour less water into the second bottle? How about more water?

You Need

- Permanent marker
- Metric ruler
- 2 clear 2-liter plastic bottles, cleaned and with labels removed
- Scissors
- Drill or sharp object (like a nail)
- Tape
- Straight drinking straw
- Modeling clay or dough
- Stopwatch

1. Use the permanent marker to make a dot about 10 centimeters from the bottom of each bottle.

2. Use the marker to draw lines 10, 15, 20, and 25 centimeters from the bottom of each bottle.

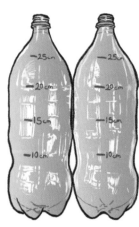

3. Ask an adult to help you use the scissors to cut the top off each 2-liter bottle.

4. With help from an adult, use a drill or other sharp object to make a hole where you made the dot on each bottle. The holes need to be big enough so the straw can fit tightly into them. Put a little tape around the edges of each hole so they are not sharp.

5. Connect the bottles by putting the ends of the straw in each hole. Use the modeling clay or dough to seal the straw into each bottle.

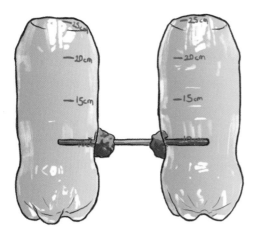

6. Place the entire setup into the sink or tub with one bottle beneath the faucet. Fill one bottle with water until it is a few centimeters higher than the level of the straw. The water should move through the straw without leaking. If it does, you're ready to experiment!

7. Empty all the water out of both bottles. Fill one bottle with water until it is level with the straw (10 cm). Get your stopwatch ready.

8. Carefully rotate the setup (or move the faucet) to fill the other bottle with water until it reaches the top. Time how long it takes the water level to become the same in both bottles.

How It Works:
Wind blows when the air pressure in one place is higher than in another. Wind is air moving from an area of higher pressure to an area of lower pressure. Often, if air pressure is the same in two places, then the air is still. The bigger the difference in air pressure, the faster the wind blows. In this experiment, water acts like air. When there is a big difference in the amount of water between the two bottles, the water moves more quickly than if there is a smaller difference. ■

How Does Rain Fall from the Sky?

YOU KNOW THAT WATER IS IN THE rivers, oceans, and lakes you see— but did you know that it is in the air, too? Water is everywhere!

That's because water can change into different forms. When hot water evaporates from large bodies like lakes or the ocean, it turns into warm, moist air. Warm air rises high into the sky, where it cools and the vapor turns back into water droplets. These droplets can hang around for a long time—that is, until they get too large and become heavy. Then, the droplets fall back down to the earth as rain. At a freezing temperature, water turns into a solid—ice. Ice that forms high in the sky can melt back to rain as it falls into warmer air. Most rain actually starts as snow in the sky before hitting the ground!

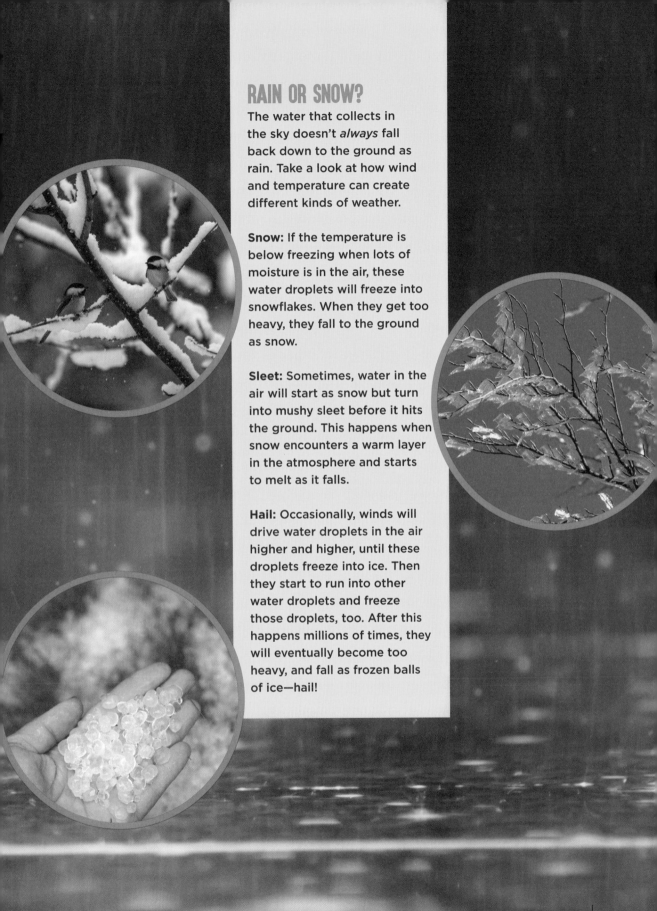

RAIN OR SNOW?

The water that collects in the sky doesn't *always* fall back down to the ground as rain. Take a look at how wind and temperature can create different kinds of weather.

Snow: If the temperature is below freezing when lots of moisture is in the air, these water droplets will freeze into snowflakes. When they get too heavy, they fall to the ground as snow.

Sleet: Sometimes, water in the air will start as snow but turn into mushy sleet before it hits the ground. This happens when snow encounters a warm layer in the atmosphere and starts to melt as it falls.

Hail: Occasionally, winds will drive water droplets in the air higher and higher, until these droplets freeze into ice. Then they start to run into other water droplets and freeze those droplets, too. After this happens millions of times, they will eventually become too heavy, and fall as frozen balls of ice—hail!

MAKE IT RAIN

Do this experiment to create your own rain at home!

You Need

- Nearly boiling water
- Clear, heatproof glass bowl
- Glass plate or lid that covers the bowl
- Ice cubes

More Ideas

When water condenses on the outside of a cold cup on a warm day, does that water come from the inside of the cup or from the air? Find out by filling two small cups (glass works best) with ice water. Cover the top of the glass with a piece of plastic wrap or a lid. Does water condense on both glasses, or just the one that's uncovered?

1. Ask an adult to pour a few inches of the nearly boiling water into the glass bowl.

2. Place the plate or the upside-down lid on the bowl.

3. Set a few ice cubes on top of the lid. Watch as water vapor condenses on the lid and "rains" back down. Gently swirl the water to see better.

How It Works:

When water is very warm, it evaporates and becomes water vapor. Water vapor rises until it hits an object called an *aerosol particle*, such as a speck of dust high in the sky. The water cools and condenses back into a droplet. Rain occurs when water droplets join together until they're too heavy to stay up, so they fall. Here, the hot water in the bowl turns into water vapor and rises until it hits the cool lid, where water droplets form, join together, and fall.

Easy

WHIPPED CREAM CLOUD

Make a whipped cream "cloud" that "rains down" food coloring!

You Need

- Measuring cup
- Water
- Food coloring (any color)
- Medium or large jar or glass
- Whipped cream (the kind that comes in a can)
- Eyedropper, straw, or plastic pipette

1. Measure half a cup of water in the measuring cup.

2. Mix a few drops of food coloring into the water. This is your "rain."

3. Fill the jar or glass three-fourths full with cool water.

4. Squirt the whipped cream into the jar or glass until it is a little higher than the top. This is your "cloud."

5. Use the eyedropper, straw, or pipette to draw up some of the rain.

6. Gently drizzle the rain on the whipped cream cloud. Wait a minute, and watch.

7. Add more rain to the cloud until the you see color in the jar. You've made it rain!

How It Works:

The whipped cream can hold on to, or *absorb*, some of the colored water. After a while, though, it can't hold any more. When this happens, the water trickles through the cloud and falls into the water below.

Clouds form when the air is saturated with water vapor. The tiny drops that make up a cloud sometimes stick together. Bigger drops get pulled on more by gravity than smaller drops do. Eventually enough drops stick together to make drops big enough that gravity will make them fall to the ground. ■

Did You Know

Raindrops aren't really tear-shaped—they start out like round balls, and then become the shape of a jelly bean or kidney bean as they fall and collide with other drops. Once they grow too large, they break apart into smaller balls again.

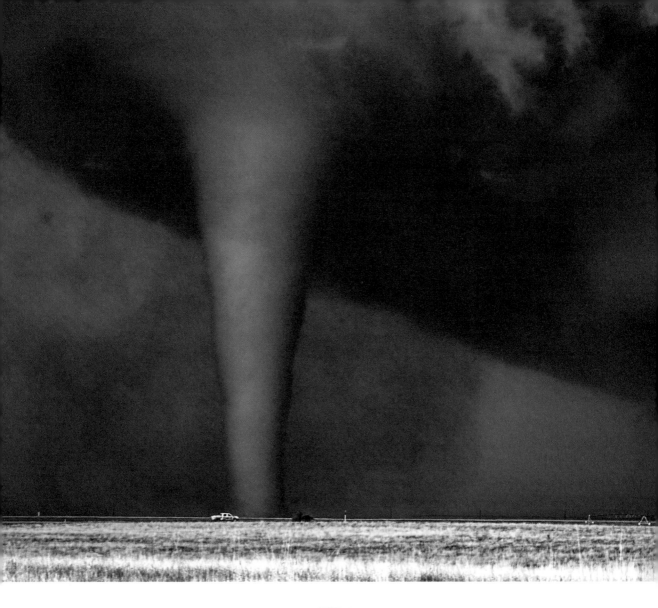

How Does a Tornado Start and Stop?

ONE OF THE MOST DANGEROUS forms of weather is a tornado. These spinning columns of air—also called twisters—usually form from certain types of thunderstorms.

When moist, warm air quickly rises from the ground to meet cool, dry air in the sky, this can create a thunderstorm. Strong winds can sometimes turn a thunderstorm into a *supercell thunderstorm*, a type of storm that rotates horizontally. As this storm starts to spin faster and faster, it sometimes meets with more air rising from the ground.

WATCHING THE WEATHER

From rain to sunshine to tornadoes to hail, there are so many kinds of weather. Luckily, scientists have developed lots of different tools that let them monitor Earth's atmosphere to try to determine what kind of weather might happen where. Some of these tools—satellites—are even in outer space. Satellites collect data as they orbit the planet, which scientists then interpret.

Other scientists use weather balloons to track temperatures, atmospheric pressure, moisture, and more. Then, advanced computer programs help them put all the data together to help figure out what kind of weather we'll see next.

A funnel-shaped column of swirling air starts to form as the storm sucks up more and more air—sometimes growing longer until it touches the ground. This is a tornado.

Unlike a supercell tornado, which can go on for hours, most tornados last less than 10 minutes. But they can still be strong enough to toss cars and destroy homes. Fortunately, when a tornado moves over cold air that doesn't rise like hot air does, it can weaken and stop. Other times, the storm above can break up, bringing an end to the tornado.

SPARKLY TORNADO

In a tornado, air spins around a central point in a shape called a *vortex*. Make your own water vortex in this experiment.

You Need

- 2 clear plastic 2-liter bottles, cleaned and with labels removed
- Water
- Liquid dish soap
- Eco-friendly glitter
- Metal or plastic washer the same size as the bottle opening
- Duct tape

1. Fill one bottle with water until it is almost full. Add two squirts of liquid dish soap and a big pinch of glitter.

2. Place the washer over the opening of the bottle full of water.

3. Tear off a piece of duct tape.

4. Turn over the empty bottle. Put its opening on top of the opening of the full bottle. Make sure the two bottle openings and the washer are all lined up.

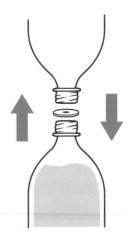

5. Use the duct tape to seal both bottles together.

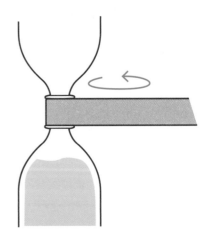

6. Hold the bottles in the middle (on the duct tape) so that the full bottle is on the bottom. Quickly flip the bottles over onto a flat surface. Grab the top bottle and move it in circles as the water starts to empty into the bottom bottle.

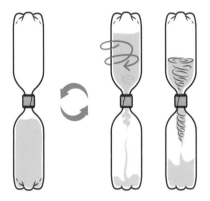

More Ideas

Add colored lamp oil to the water bottle to see what happens—how does the vortex change? Add small objects like beads to your bottle. What happens to them during the vortex?

7. Watch your vortex form as the water moves into the empty bottle.

How It Works:

The water vortex in this experiment forms when you spin the bottle. The water on the outside of the vortex is moving more slowly than the water in the center of the vortex. This gives the vortex the swirled pattern you observe. In a tornado, the vortex is made of air moving around a center point. The air on the outside of the tornado moves more slowly than the air right around its center, giving tornadoes their funnel-like appearance. ■

How Do Rainbows Form?

IF RAINBOWS SEEM MAGICAL, IT'S because they sort of are! Rainbows are optical illusions—a type of image that tricks our brains—formed by moisture and light.

After it rains, or when water sprays from a fountain or hose, lots of water hangs in the air. If sunlight hits these droplets of water at just the right angle, the light scatters. This only happens when the sun is in the opposite end of the sky from the droplets—so if you are looking at a rainbow, the sun will always be behind you.

Sunlight does not normally appear as color because it is white. But white light is actually made up of all colors. When the sunlight scatters, it is split up into its separate colors. To us, this looks like a rainbow. However, rainbows don't actually exist in one place. Because a rainbow is made of light, its appearance and position can vary slightly depending on where a person is standing. Plus, rainbows are actually circles! Humans can only see half of this circle, as the other half is below the horizon. After the raindrops fall from the air or the sun moves its position, the rainbow will disappear—just like magic.

Sunlight hitting raindrops in the air scatters, reflecting back to the viewer as different colors.

MAKE A RAINBOW

Make a little colorful rainbow magic with this simple experiment.

You Need

- White paper
- A sunny windowsill
- Small clear glass
- Water

1. Put the paper down on the windowsill or other flat spot in bright sun.

2. Fill the glass a little over halfway with water.

3. Put the glass on the paper.

4. If you don't see a rainbow, carefully pick up the glass and lift it slowly straight up.

How It Works:

The sunlight we see has all the colors mixed together in it. When light moves through water, it *refracts*, or bends. Each drop of water acts like a tiny prism, splitting the light into all the colors of the rainbow. ■

Tip

If your rainbow isn't very bright, tip the glass a little in the sunlight.

More Ideas

Make a rainbow using a garden hose. Just squeeze the hose handle gently so that the water comes out in a fine mist. Stand with the sun behind you and point the water in different directions until your rainbow is bright and colorful.

Did You Know?

The light of the moon can also be refracted through water droplets. When this happens (which is rarely!) the result is called a moonbow.

THE
OCEAN

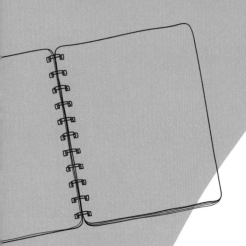

Quick Challenges

The ocean is many shades of blue and green. List as many different shades of blue and green as you can think of.

Research one thing you can do to help keep the ocean clean.

Put a pillow at your feet. Then take 40 steps in a straight line away from the pillow. You've just walked about the length of a blue whale!

Use aluminum foil to make a boat, and then float it in water. For extra fun, see how many paper clips it can hold before it sinks.

Make model ocean currents by sprinkling some cornmeal or flour over a mixing bowl full of water and blowing across the top of the water.

Draw your favorite ocean animal.

How Deep Is the Ocean?

IMAGINE A ROLLING LANDSCAPE, with deep canyons and tall mountains. Now, imagine it completely covered in water. You're picturing the ocean floor!

The ocean doesn't have just one depth, because the ocean floor has hills, flat stretches, valleys, and more, just like dry land. Some parts, like many places near the shore where the ocean ends and dry land begins, are very shallow. Others, like deep trenches, are very, very deep.

Scientists who have mapped the ocean floor have calculated that, on average, the ocean is just over two miles deep.

But the deepest part of the ocean, the Mariana Trench in the Pacific Ocean, is almost seven miles deep!

Scientists figure out ocean depths using something called *sonar*, which is a method of creating an image of something using just sound. During this process, a ship sends out sound waves to the bottom of the ocean, and then measures how long it takes for the sound waves to return. In this way, they can use computers to create a map of the ocean floor—just like we have for dry land.

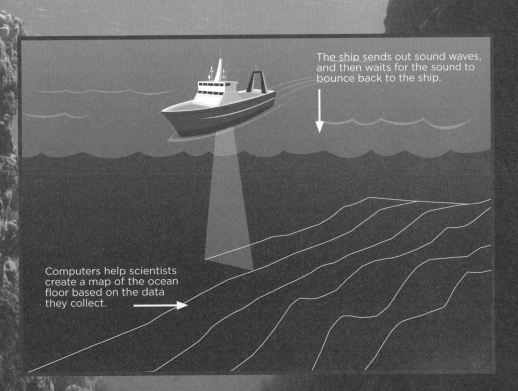

The ship sends out sound waves, and then waits for the sound to bounce back to the ship.

Computers help scientists create a map of the ocean floor based on the data they collect.

MAPPING THE OCEAN FLOOR

Oceanographers study everything about the ocean, including its bottom, or floor—but it's too deep to see with just our eyes. How can you make a map of something without seeing it? Find out in this activity.

You Need

- Modeling clay or dough
- Shoebox with a lid
- Tape
- Graph paper (larger squares are better for this activity)
- Safety goggles
- Thin wooden skewer
- Metric ruler
- Colored pencils or markers: red, orange, yellow, green, blue, purple, brown, and pink

1. Use the modeling clay or dough to make a section of ocean floor in the bottom of the shoebox (Hint: Parts of the seafloor look like a mountain range, with lots of high peaks and low valleys.). Allow the clay or dough to dry until it's hard to the touch.

2. Tape a piece of graph paper to the outside top of the lid, and then tape the lid to the shoebox.

3. Put on the safety goggles. Lay the skewer next to the metric ruler and measure 16 centimeters on the skewer, marking off every two centimeters with a black dot. Use markers to color the space up to the first dot red, the space up to the second dot orange, and so on, creating a guide that matches the color key shown here. ➡

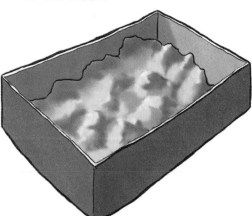

Tip

Some parts of the ocean are very deep, and some are very shallow. Model your ocean floor the same way, piling the clay high in some places, and making other areas low.

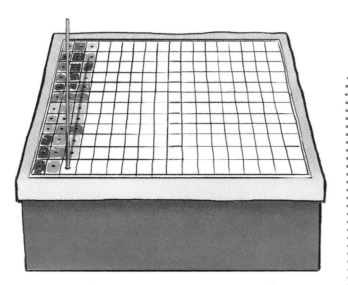

Sonar

Oceanographers use sonar to map the bottom of the ocean. Sonar works because of echoes. Ships send a sound down to the ocean floor and record how long it takes to get back to the ship. A computer assigns a color to each depth and displays the different depths in a map.

4. Poke the skewer into a square on the graph paper and through the lid of the shoebox until it touches the clay ocean floor. What color on the skewer lines up with the top of the box? Grab that color pencil or marker. Remove the skewer, and use the pencil or marker to color the square.

5. Keep testing squares until you have a map of your ocean floor. ∎

More Ideas

Use your finished map to trace a route over the deepest parts of your ocean.

Did You Know?

People aren't the only living things that use sonar in the sea. Some animals, like orcas and dolphins, use a special kind of sonar called echolocation (see page 84) to track down fish to eat.

How Far Can Ocean Waves Travel?

IF YOU'VE EVER VISITED A beach, the waves you've seen might have traveled for thousands of miles before crashing onto the shore in front of you. Or, they may have just been created then and there!

Most of the ocean's waves are formed by energy from the wind. Sometimes, the wind or a breeze just forms ripples over the water's surface. Other times, a huge storm occurs over the ocean. When that happens, a lot of energy pushes the water into huge waves.

Once they're formed, waves don't stop until they run into something. They may stop growing if the storm dies down, but they will keep traveling in the same direction. This means that if a large storm formed far out at sea, the waves it created might travel for thousands of miles.

A wave's energy will stop once it hits, or breaks on, something. Most of the time, this is the ocean shore. As waves approach the shore, the ground gets shallower. The water carried at the bottom of the wave starts to get caught up on the shallow shoreline, becoming slower. But the top of the wave keeps going! Because the top of the wave is moving faster than the bottom, it eventually falls over itself, forming the crashing waves you see at the beach.

WILD WAVES

Not all waves are caused by the wind. Sometimes, an earthquake or a volcano sends out huge amounts of energy into the ocean. This can cause enormous waves, or even tsunamis. A tsunami can happen when a blast of energy pushes huge amounts of water out of place. This causes an extremely large wave, or even series of waves, that can become more than 100 feet tall. Luckily, scientists have ways of detecting ocean movement that could trigger tsunamis, which lets them send out warnings to people living on the shore.

OCEAN IN A BOTTLE

Earth's oceans are always in motion. What kind of motion? Waves. Make a wave in a bottle in this activity.

You Need

- Funnel (optional)
- 16- or 20-ounce water bottle with cap, label removed
- Water
- Blue food coloring
- Vegetable oil

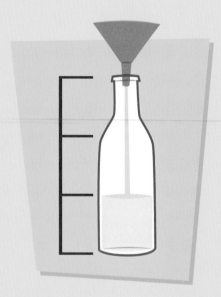

1. Use the funnel to help you fill the bottle about one-third full with water.

2. Add 4–5 drops of food coloring and swirl gently to mix.

3. Hold the bottle between both hands horizontally. Slowly rock (or tilt) the bottle one way and then the other. Observe the wave. How fast does it move?

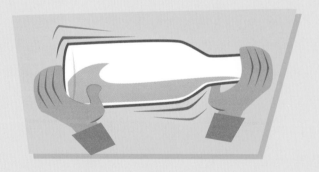

4. Remove the cap and use the funnel to fill the rest of the bottle to the top with vegetable oil. Put the cap back on the bottle.

5. Hold the bottle between both hands horizontally. Slowly rock (or tilt) the bottle one way and then the other. Observe your wave again—how fast does it move?

How It Works:
Water and oil don't mix because they have different densities. The clear line between the two liquids helps you to see how energy is carried along in a wave. ▪

More Ideas

Do steps 1–3 to create another ocean bottle. Instead of adding oil, drop a piece of wax into the bottle. Hold the bottle horizontally again and make a wave. What happens to the wax?

How Did the Ocean Get So Salty?

THE OCEAN MIGHT LOOK LIKE IT could quench your thirst, but it is definitely not good for humans to drink. That's because it's full of salt!

When the ocean first formed nearly four billion years ago, it may have only been a little salty. But that has changed, thanks to rivers and rain. As rain falls across the planet, it washes over mountains, rocks, and the earth, which are all made of minerals. Over many years, rains can wear these things down. Rocks break open and mountains *erode*, or start to crumble away. Then the rain washes their minerals into rivers and streams.

These rivers and streams don't seem salty because the water in them is constantly running and being replenished by rains and mountain snow. But most of these rivers and streams flow into the sea, where all the minerals collect. Over billions of years, the ocean has collected enough minerals to become salty.

This doesn't mean that the ocean is still getting saltier, though. Much of the salt in the ocean settles as small pieces called *sediment* on the ocean floor. But thanks to the constant flow from rivers, it isn't losing salt either—so it won't be good to drink anytime soon.

SURVIVING IN SALT

If we were to live surrounded by salt like lots of marine animals do, it would make us sick. But these animals have special adaptations that help them thrive in salty seas. Many fish are able to get rid of some of the salt they take in through their internal organs, which collect the salt as a waste product and release it as urine. Some fish also have special cells in their gills that can get rid of salt.

Did You Know

Ocean *currents* are continuous movements of water in a particular direction. The level of salt in the ocean and changes in density help make deep-ocean currents happen. For example, winds cause warm surface water from the equator to flow north. The water cools and becomes denser as it moves farther away from the equator. In certain spots, some of the water freezes, leaving behind extra salt in the ocean. This makes the water even denser, causing it to sink. New water then flows in to fill the space. This cycle helps keep a deep-ocean current on the move!

Easy

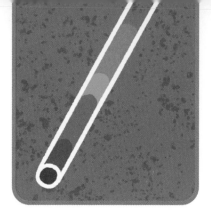

SALTWATER RAINBOW

Different densities of saltwater in the ocean help to make deep-ocean currents. (See the "Did You Know?" on page 195.) Find out how different densities of saltwater can make layers in this colorful experiment.

You Need

- Scissors
- Paper
- Marker
- Tape
- 6 clear glass cups that can hold at least 8 ounces (1 cup) of water and are at least 6 inches tall (taller, thinner cups work best)
- Teaspoon
- Table salt
- Food coloring
- 1-cup measuring cup
- Warm water
- Mixing spoon
- Clear drinking straw

1. Use the scissors to cut out paper labels for your cups. Number the labels 1 through 6 and tape the labels to the cups.

2. Use the table on this page to see how much salt and food coloring to add to each cup.

3. Use the measuring cup to add one cup of warm water to each cup. Stir each cup carefully to mix.

4. Lower the clear drinking straw about an inch into cup 1. Place your thumb over the top of the straw.

5. Keeping your thumb over the top of the straw, move the straw into cup 2. This time, dip the straw about one inch deeper into the liquid.

6. Lift your thumb, then press it firmly over the top of the straw again.

7. Repeat steps 5 and 6 for the rest of the cups.

8. Admire your rainbow!

How It Works:

Density is a measure of mass divided by volume. Each cup of water has a different density because you've added a different mass of salt to the same volume of water. Cup 6 has the highest density because it has the most salt. Cup 1 has the lowest density because it has the least salt. The different colors of water make layers because liquids that have a lower density float on top of liquids that have a higher density.

Cup	Salt	Food Coloring
1	1 tsp	4 drops red
2	2 tsp	2 drops red, 2 drops yellow
3	3 tsp	4 drops yellow
4	4 tsp	4 drops green
5	5 tsp	4 drops blue
6	6 tsp	2 drops red, 2 drops blue

FLOATING GRAPE EXPERIMENT

Things float much more easily in the ocean than in a lake or river. Find out why in this simple but "grape" experiment.

Tip
The bigger the grape, the more salt you will need.

5. Carefully drop the grape into the salty water. Do you notice anything different? If not, use the spoon to scoop out the grape and add more salt.

How It Works:
The grape sank in the glass the first time because grapes are more dense than water. Adding salt to the water made the liquid inside the cup more dense than the grape, so the grape floated when you dropped it into the glass the second time. ■

You Need

- Clear drinking glass
- Warm water
- Grape
- Spoon
- Teaspoon
- Table salt

1. Fill the glass with warm water.

2. Drop the grape into the glass. Observe what happens.

3. Use the spoon to scoop the grape out of the glass and put it aside.

4. Add three teaspoons of salt to the water. Stir to mix until the salt is dissolved.

How Do Coral Reefs Grow?

CORALS MIGHT LOOK LIKE beautiful rocks or plants, but they're actually small sea animals! A coral's body is known as a *polyp*. At the top of the polyp is the coral's mouth, often surrounded by small tentacles. This is the colorful, plantlike part you might see fluttering in the water.

When a coral is a baby (known as a *larva*), it swims through the ocean until it finds a good place for a home, such as a rock. Some coral, such as sea fans, do not develop hard outer structures. These soft corals do not form reefs.

Other corals secrete a mineral called calcium carbonate. As the mineral builds, it forms a hard, protective covering for their bodies. These hard corals create the reefs we see and provide a place for other coral larvae to land and build on! As they grow, coral reefs become ecosystems and homes for many different ocean animals—the largest one is nearly 1,500 miles long! Animals living in coral reefs have food and safe places to hide—all thanks to the tiny coral.

PROTECTING CORAL REEFS

Coral reefs are incredibly important; they are home to many kinds of ocean life. They also take a long time to form. Just one coral reef can take 10,000 years to form—and even up to 30 million years, depending on its size! Because of that, it's important to protect coral reefs. Here are some things you can do to help keep them safe:

• Use reef-friendly sunscreen when swimming.
• Recycle and don't litter—most litter ends up in the ocean.
• Pollution from cars harms oceans and reefs. So instead of driving, encourage friends and family to walk, bike, or ride the bus whenever possible.
• Have an adult help you write to your local representative to urge them to help protect reefs.

EDIBLE POLYPS

When we look at a coral reef, we see lots of individual corals growing next to one another. Learn more about how a reef forms by making a bunch of these individuals, called *polyps*.

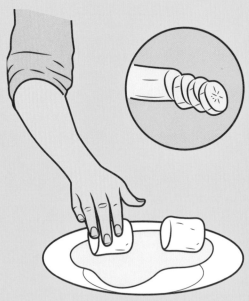

You Need

- Paper plate
- White chocolate, white chocolate chips, or white candy wafers
- Small microwavable bowl or small saucepan
- 4 large marshmallows or banana cut into 4 chunks
- Toothpick
- 6 thin pieces of red licorice (rope-style licorice works best) per marshmallow
- Candy sprinkles

1. Start building your coral reef: Set the paper plate on the table. The paper plate represents the limestone found at the base of many reefs.

2. Put the white chocolate in the bowl. Ask an adult to help you melt the white chocolate using a heat source or microwave.

3. Each marshmallow or banana chunk represents a coral polyp's body. Roll each body in the chocolate coating so the sides are covered. When the coating hardens, it's a good representation of the hard limestone skeleton that many corals have.

4. Place the coated marshmallows or banana chunks close to each other on the paper plate. Polyps grow very close to each other on a reef when they form colonies.

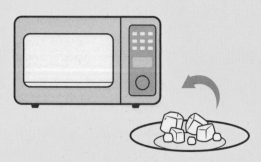

5. Use the toothpick to poke six evenly spaced holes in a circle around the top of each marshmallow or banana chunk.

6. Insert one thin piece of licorice in each hole. These represent a polyp's tentacles, used to pull food into the growing polyp's mouth.

7. Sprinkle a tiny bit of water on the top of the polyps, and gently add sprinkles to the top of each. These represent zooxanthellae.

8. After you're done admiring your model—eat it! ■

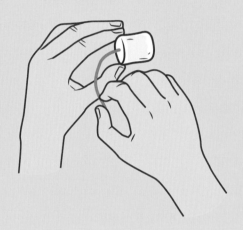
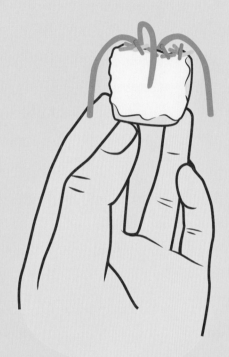

What are zooxanthellae?

Zooxanthellae are tiny plantlike organisms, or algae, that live inside the coral polyp. Algae use sunlight to live and grow, like plants do. They share some of their energy with the coral. In return, the coral polyp provides a home and food for the zooxanthellae.

How Does Seafoam Form?

AFTER A WAVE CRASHES ONTO the shore, you might notice foamy white bubbles clinging to the sand. Other times, you might see this frothy foam swirling on top of the moving water.

Have you ever stopped to wonder exactly what this seafoam is? It might seem like the bubbles that form in a bubble bath, but there's more to it than that. If you examined a glass of water that you filled up in the sink, it would probably be mostly clear. But if you studied a glass of seawater, it would look much cloudier.

This is because seawater is full of salt, sand, and other minerals. It is also full of life! Even though you probably wouldn't be able to see it without a

microscope, that glass of seawater would be full of tiny organisms that call the ocean home. And some of these organisms, called *algae*, help create seafoam.

Algae are plantlike organisms that live in the water and use the sun to create their own food in a process called *photosynthesis*. When algae break down, they give off tiny particles of proteins, fats, and other minerals that dissolve into the water. Then, when waves, wind, or other disturbances stir up all these particles, they churn into a frothy white foam.

Most of this foam swirls on top of the water or at the edges of waves. But if there has been lots of algae present in the water, it might mix into a thick foam that lasts a while longer—and looks a lot more like bubble bath bubbles!

AMAZING ALGAE

There are many different kinds of algae all over the world. Some algae, such as seaweed or kelp, are large enough for you to easily spot. Other algae are so tiny that they are invisible to the human eye. No matter the size, algae is super important for life on Earth. For some animals, large forests of seaweed and kelp can provide safe homes or places to find food. Other animals depend on the algae itself for their meals. And on top of that, algae provides a huge amount of oxygen for the planet!

FROTHY FOAM FUN

Recreate the fluffy foam that caps many of the ocean's waves and collects on shore with a few simple ingredients.

You Need

- Milk (about 1 cup)
- Heat-safe glass jar with a lid
- Packet of hot cocoa mix (without marshmallows)
- Oven mitts
- Mug

1. Read the directions on the hot cocoa package to find out how much milk you need to make one serving. Place that much milk into the glass jar.

2. Ask an adult to help you heat the milk in the microwave. (This is usually best done by setting the microwave on medium-high, and then heating for 15 seconds at a time, stirring between each heating. The milk is heated enough when it is warm but not hot or boiling.)

Safety Tip

The lid of the jar may be metal. Do not put the lid on the jar of milk before you microwave it!

3. With an adult's help, put on oven mitts and remove the jar from the microwave. (It will be hot.) Then pour the hot chocolate mix into the jar.

4. Put the lid on the jar tightly. Shake the jar until all the mix is dissolved.

How It Works:
Milk gets foamy when it's stirred or shaken up because it contains proteins. The proteins surround pockets of air to make bubbles. Seawater also has proteins in it, along with fats and minerals, which come from algae breaking down in the water. When waves and wind force air into the ocean water, bubbles can form around these particles, just as they do in the milk. ■

5. Carefully pour the liquid into a mug and observe the foam on top!

How Do Marine Animals Stay Warm?

BRRR—THE OCEAN CAN BE A chilly place. This is especially true in freezing areas like Antarctica! Luckily for them, the marine animals that live in these places have clever ways of staying warm.

Some animals, like many fish, are able to survive cold months by slowing down their body functions and using less energy. There are some fish, like some sharks, that can raise the temperatures of their bodies by swimming, thanks to special blood vessels. And other fish—like the ones that live in the ocean's freezing depths—actually have special antifreeze substances in their blood.

But what about mammals? Most marine animals—from whales to seals to walruses—have a thick layer of fat called *blubber*. This blubber traps heat, keeping the animals nice and toasty. On top of that, it acts as a storage place for energy, and even helps marine mammals float!

PENGUIN PARTY

Penguins aren't mammals, but they have blubber, too! But sometimes, icy temperatures where these birds live are too cold for blubber alone. Luckily, penguins also have thick feathers that trap heat against their skin. And if they're still cold? They cuddle! Penguins huddle together in large groups to share body heat and stay warm.

BLUBBER MITTEN

Many mammals that live in icy water have thick fat called *blubber* to help keep them warm. Feel how it works for yourself in this activity!

2. Scoop several heaping spoonfuls of shortening into the two quart-sized plastic bags. Zip the bags closed.

1. Fill the bowl about half full with water and ice. Set the bowl aside.

3. Use your hands to pat the shortening inside the bags into an even layer. The layer should be about one inch thick. If it isn't, add more shortening and pat flat again.

4. Stack the shortening-filled bags one on top of the other. Use the duct tape to seal three sides of the bags together. Leave the other side open so you can put your hand between the layers.

5. Slide your hand in between the taped-together bags. Then, put the gallon-sized bag over the top of the whole thing—two bags, hand, and all.

6. Put your hand with the blubber mitten on it into the bowl of ice water. How long does it take before it starts to feel really cold?

How It Works:
Blubber is a fat. So is shortening. Fats are good at keeping in heat. Just like blubber helps many marine mammals stay warm in cold ocean water, the shortening helps trap heat around your hand in the bowl of ice water. ■

More Ideas

See if it makes a difference how quickly your hand gets cold if the shortening layer is thicker or thinner than one inch. Try other materials instead of shortening in the bags.

Did You Know?

Mammals and birds have to keep their body temperatures about the same all the time. Fish, reptiles, and amphibians don't.

OUTER SPACE

Quick Challenges

How many other words can you make from the word *asteroid*? Set a timer for three minutes and see what you come up with.

Join marshmallows with toothpicks to make a star constellation.

Invent your own planet. Draw a picture of what it looks like from space and what it looks like on the surface.

Make an astronaut helmet from an old box.

Use all of the names of the planets in our solar system (Mercury, Venus, Earth, Mars, Jupiter, Saturn, Uranus, and Neptune) in a story.

Imagine you're in charge of designing a new spaceship. Draw your design and give the spaceship a name.

How Did the Moon Form?

ON MOST CLEAR NIGHTS, YOU CAN see the moon above you. But, according to some scientists, it probably wasn't always there—long ago, Earth likely had no moon.

Experts aren't sure how the moon formed, but they do have theories based on what they know about space and how planets and rocky celestial bodies (like asteroids) form. Most scientists believe in something called the *giant impact hypothesis*. This theory states that billions of years ago, there were more planets in our solar system—including a Mars-size planet that scientists have named Theia. So where did this planet go? Long before any people or animals existed, it crashed into Earth! Scientists think that a giant collision between the two planets sent enormous chunks of rock flying into space, where gravity drew them together to form the moon you see now.

According to other scientists though, the moon may have existed before it was tied to Earth's gravity. In this scenario, called the *capture theory*, scientists think that a passing rocky body—the moon—may have traveled too close to Earth and gotten stuck in its orbit.

On the other hand, some scientists believe that the moon *might* have always been there. The *co-formation theory* says that the moon and Earth formed together in the early days of the solar system. Though scientists believe that the moon will eventually break free of Earth's gravity and drift out of orbit, it's not going anywhere anytime soon.

DESIGN A MOON PHASE CALENDAR

Every month, the moon goes through a pattern of phases. They make the moon look like it's changing shape (but it's not). Learn the pattern and the name of each phase by making a calendar.

You Need

- Blue poster board or 3 pieces of blue construction paper with the short ends taped together
- Cup or glass
- Pen or marker
- White poster board or construction paper
- Black poster board or construction paper
- Scissors
- Glue stick
- Tape (optional)

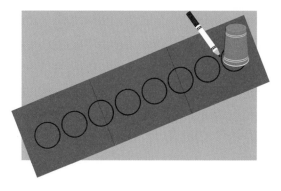

2. With the marker, trace around the cup to make eight circles in a row across the blue poster board or strip of construction paper.

1. If you are using poster board, lay it horizontally on your work area. If you are using construction paper, tape three pieces of blue construction paper together to make a strip.

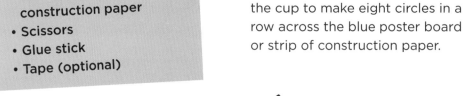

3. Trace four circles on the white poster board or construction paper and one circle on the black poster board or construction paper. Cut these out.

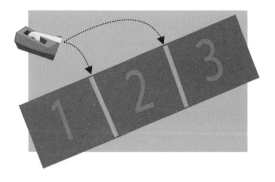

More Ideas

Keep a moon journal. Look for the moon every day and night for a month and draw its shape in a journal.

★☆☆
Easy

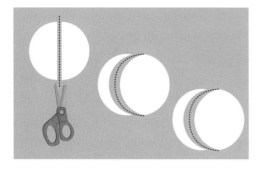

4. Cut one of the white circles in half and cut crescent shapes from two of the other white circles.

5. Use the picture at the bottom of this page to help you place the pieces of your calendar together. Glue each moon phase to the correct spot on the poster board or strip of construction paper.

6. Write the name of each phase below the correct shape. ■

Phases of the Moon

Earth's moon doesn't actually change shape—it just looks like it does to us on Earth. As our moon orbits Earth, different parts are lit up by the sun's light. When the dark side of the moon is facing Earth, we say the moon is new. As the moon enters the sun's light, we see it as a crescent. As the moon continues to move, more of the sun's light hits it, so it appears to get bigger, and we say the moon is waxing. We see a full moon when the whole side of the moon is lit up. As the moon moves out of the sun's light, we see less of the moon, and it appears to get smaller, or wane.

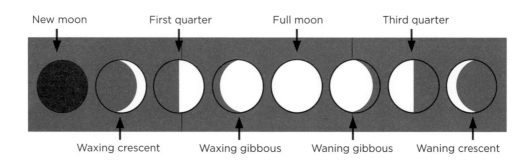

New moon   First quarter   Full moon   Third quarter

Waxing crescent   Waxing gibbous   Waning gibbous   Waning crescent

How Does the Sun Heat Earth?

EVEN IF YOU COULD SOMEHOW travel to the sun in a heatproof space-ship, you'd still encounter lots of problems—including having nowhere to land. This is because the sun is made entirely of incredibly hot gas.

The two main gases that make up the sun are called hydrogen and helium. Hydrogen makes up about 91% of the sun. Deep down in the center of the sun, this gas is super-hot. Tiny units of hydrogen known as molecules crash into each other in super-energetic collisions. When that happens, these molecules join together. When they join, they create helium. This process is called *nuclear fusion*, and it makes a lot of energy.

The sun gives off its energy as light, also known as *electromagnetic radiation*. Many types of electromagnetic radiation travel from the sun. Some of this light—such as ultraviolet (UV) radiation—can be harmful to humans. Luckily for us, the atmosphere around Earth absorbs most of the UV light, and only a small amount gets through. (Some of the light that trickles through can still cause damage though, which is why it's good to wear sunscreen.) Other types of electromagnetic radiation can regularly make their way through the atmosphere to Earth's surface. When the radiation travels through our atmosphere, it soon reaches the ground and the ocean. The earth and the water collect this energy, holding on to it and becoming warmer. This heats up the planet. The atmosphere around our planet also helps to "trap" heat in, keeping Earth warm.

As Earth spins on its axis, electro-magnetic radiation only hits the parts of the planet that are facing the sun (or the areas where it's daytime). The parts of the planet facing away from the sun (where it's nighttime) do not receive any radiation. These areas lose some of the heat that had been stored during the day. This is why nighttime is colder than daytime. Without the sun, Earth would be a very cold place indeed. How cold? According to some estimates, if the sun disappeared, temperatures on Earth would become so frigid that the entire ocean would freeze solid!

SUN SHADES

When its light travels through our thick atmosphere, the sun often looks orange or yellow to us. But our sun is actually what is known as a white star. And other suns—the stars you see at night—are different colors! The stars with the coolest temperatures are the red and orange stars. And the hottest stars are the blue ones.

SOLAR S'MORES

Use rays from the sun to create a tasty, toasted treat—s'mores!

Tip

The activities on these pages work best on a warm, sunny day.

You Need

- Small table or chair
- Aluminum foil
- Graham crackers
- Bar of chocolate
- Large marshmallows
- Magnifying glass

1. Set up a small table or chair outside in the sun. This will be your workstation.

2. Tear off a piece of aluminum foil about six inches long. Fold the aluminum foil in half, and then unfold the foil.

3. Start piecing together your first s'more by stacking one graham cracker, a square of chocolate, and a marshmallow on one half of the aluminum foil.

4. Fold the other half of the foil so that it directs the sun's light onto the marshmallow.

5. Hold the magnifying glass between the foil and the marshmallow to turn up the heat.

6. When the marshmallow is toasted, put another graham cracker on top of your s'more and enjoy!

Safety Tip

Make sure you put sunscreen on before you start this experiment (and any time you go outside!). Do not use the magnifying glass to direct light anywhere except on the marshmallow.

SUN PRINTS

Shadows usually disappear when the sun goes down—but they won't in this experiment! Use the sun's rays to make shadow art!

Safety Tip
Don't forget to wear sunscreen!

You Need

- Items that can be pressed flat, like leaves
- Bright-colored construction paper
- Plastic wrap
- 4 hand-size rocks

1. Collect leaves and other items for your sun print.

2. Place the construction paper outside on a flat surface.

3. Arrange your leaves and other objects on the construction paper to create a design.

4. Place a piece of plastic wrap on top of your sun print. Smooth the plastic out as best as you can.

5. Place a rock on each corner to hold the plastic wrap in place.

6. Leave the print in the sun for 3–4 hours.

7. Remove the leaves and other items and observe your artwork.

How It Works:
Sunlight is made of lots of different kinds of light mixed together. One of these kinds of light is called *ultraviolet (UV) light*. UV light can break apart some of the chemicals that make color in construction paper and cause it to fade. It can't get through the leaves and other objects, though, so these leave a bright-colored "shadow" on the paper. ■

More Ideas
Use scissors and more construction paper to cut out the letters of your name for a new print.

How Do Eclipses Happen?

FOR THOUSANDS OF YEARS, humans have been fascinated—and sometimes even scared—by eclipses. Today, we know that eclipses are perfectly natural occurrences with no cause for alarm, although they are still amazing!

An eclipse happens when one astronomical body in our solar system, such as the moon, casts a shadow that blocks out all or part of another, such as the sun. From Earth, we can see two kinds of eclipses: solar and lunar.

When the moon is orbiting Earth, sometimes it passes directly between Earth and the sun. When this happens, the moon blocks the sun's light from getting to Earth, making it look like the sun has gone dark. This is a *solar eclipse*.

During a solar eclipse, the moon can look like it is either blocking all of the sun or only a portion. Whether you see a total eclipse or a partial one depends on where you are located on Earth in relation to the sun at the time of the event. During some solar eclipses, based on how far apart the moon and the sun are at the time, the moon can even appear to form a dark circle within an outer halo of sunlight. No matter how they appear, total solar eclipses usually only last a few minutes before Earth rotates enough so that people seeing the eclipse are moved out of the moon's shadow and can see the sun again.

A *lunar eclipse*, on the other hand, happens when Earth moves between the sun and the moon. Because the moon always orbits Earth and Earth always orbits the sun, the sun's light normally bounces off the moon in lots of different ways. This illuminates the moon for people on Earth, causing the appearance of full moons, crescent moons, and more. But during a lunar eclipse, Earth moves so that it is directly in between the sun and the moon. When this happens, a small amount of the sun's light still reaches the moon. However, it must first travel through Earth's atmosphere. This makes the moon look red to people on Earth! Total lunar eclipses can last nearly two hours. But as with a solar eclipse, the astronomical bodies keep moving, and the moon will soon go back to its normal appearance.

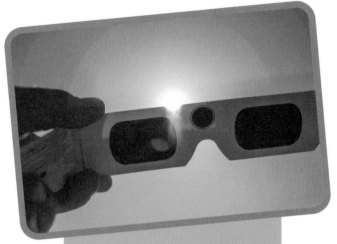

SEEING A SOLAR ECLIPSE

Solar eclipses can be beautiful and awe-inspiring, but it's important to take the right care when viewing them. If even a little bit of sunlight is peeking out from behind the moon, it is still very dangerous to look at the sun, as the sun's rays can easily damage the sensitive cells in a person's eyes. Luckily, scientists make specially filtered sunglasses that make it safe for people to view solar eclipses.

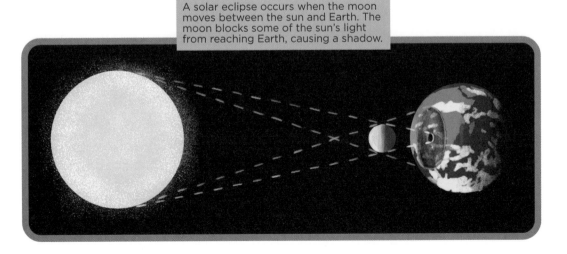

A solar eclipse occurs when the moon moves between the sun and Earth. The moon blocks some of the sun's light from reaching Earth, causing a shadow.

SOLAR ECLIPSE CRACKERS

Create a "solar eclipse" right in your home with this solar eclipse snack activity.

1. Ask an adult to help you to cut the cucumber into slices. Place these on a plate.

2. Lay out a row of six round crackers. Place a cucumber slice on top of each cracker.

3. Open a package of cream cheese. Leave the first cucumber slice with nothing on it. This represents the sun before a solar eclipse. Use the table knife to cover the last cucumber slice with cream cheese. This represents the sun when it's totally eclipsed.

4. Using the picture below to help you, spread cream cheese on the middle four slices to represent how the shape of the sun appears to change during a solar eclipse.

Safety Tip

Ask an adult to help with anything sharp.

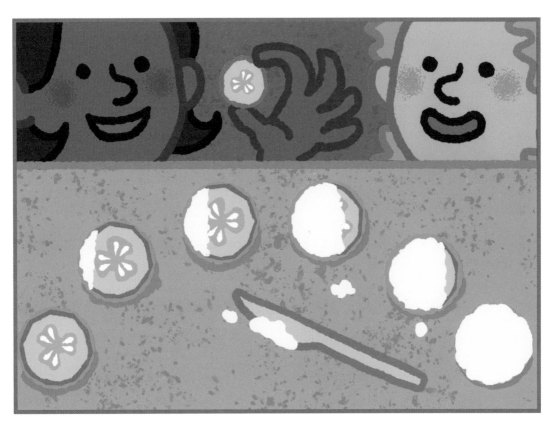

5. Make sure the crackers are arranged correctly, and then eat your way through a solar eclipse! ■

How Did We Put a Rover on Mars?

RIGHT NOW, THERE ISN'T JUST one rover on Mars—there are at least six, with more missions underway! The first one, NASA's Sojourner, landed in 1997. In 2021, NASA's Perseverance and China's Zhurong both landed on the planet.

In addition to the rovers, many landers have reached Mars over the past 50 years or so. Landers are spacecraft designed to safely land on other planets and astronomical bodies in our solar system. If they land successfully, they then begin their jobs of sending information back to Earth, all while staying in the spot they landed. Rovers, on the other hand, are designed not just to land, but also to explore. These robotic vehicles can travel across the surface of Mars, taking samples and images and collecting data. But how do they get there in the first place?

First, scientists design and build the rover. This can take years, as the scientists must take into account all the different jobs the rover has to do and all the situations it might encounter. They also have to design computer systems that can both withstand the dust storms and terrain of Mars and send data all the way back to Earth.

Then, once the rover has been built and tested, it has to be launched from Earth. Scientists do this by attaching the rover to enormous rockets. The rockets use controlled explosions to push against the earth and escape the planet's gravity (see pages 14–15). Once it's in space, the rover can be navigated remotely from Earth, using smaller rockets called thrusters that can adjust its course.

After all that comes the trickiest part: Once the rover has reached its destination, it's time to land. Landing is very difficult, as the rover could burn up in the atmosphere or crash into the planet. For this reason, rovers are built with heat shields, parachutes, airbags, and even jet packs.

As the rover descends, the shield protects it from the heat, and the atmosphere slows its fall. After its fall slows somewhat, the rover deploys a parachute, and sometimes jet packs to help slow it down even more. Finally, it bounces safely on its airbags. Welcome to Mars!

PASTA PLANET ROVER

It takes a lot of creativity to plan a vehicle designed to explore the surface of faraway planets. Can you make a working model with pasta, glue, and a few other supplies?

You Need

- Paper
- Markers
- 1 dry lasagna noodle
- Something round with a hole in the middle for wheels (wheel-shaped pasta, round candies, cookies, etc.)
- Something long for the axles (bucatini, thin pretzel sticks, etc.)
- Other types of pasta or materials to make your rover unique
- Low-heat glue gun

1. Draw a sketch of a Mars rover that can roll across the floor or down a ramp. Use the pictures on these pages as inspiration, or make up your own design. The only rules are that it has to use a lasagna noodle in its design, and it has to be able to roll.

2. Make your model—lay out all the pieces according to your design.

3. If something doesn't look like it will work, change it and fix your drawing.

4. With an adult's help, use the glue gun to assemble the pieces of your model. Go back to step 3 if necessary.

5. Test your model—does it roll? If it doesn't, go back to step 1 and try again! ■

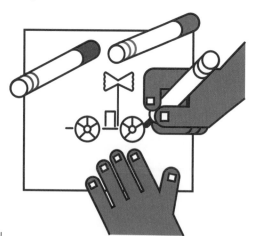

Tip

Pasta is fragile—take care when constructing your Mars rover.

Safety Tip

Always be cautious using the glue gun.

More Ideas

Build a ramp out of cardboard and books—does your model roll downhill? See if you can design and make another rover that rolls faster or farther than your first model.

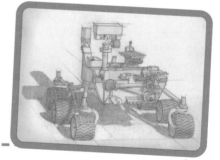

The Engineering Design Process

Have you ever heard the saying "back to the drawing board"? Engineers, people who design machines like cars and airplanes (and Mars rovers), rarely get their designs right on the first try. And if a design doesn't seem right or doesn't work, they don't give up. They try to change their plans, or, in some cases, start over completely!

How Did Saturn Get Its Rings?

SATURN IS ONE OF FOUR PLANETS in our solar system with rings. Neptune, Jupiter, and Uranus also have rings. However, Saturn's are the largest and the brightest of the bunch, which is probably why Saturn is the most famous ringed planet.

Saturn's enormous rings are made mostly from chunks of ice and rock. Some chunks are huge while others are tiny. Scientists aren't sure when these rings of ice and rock formed, but they do think they might know how.

According to some experts, the answer might lie in Saturn's many moons—the planet has more than 80! Scientists think that over many, many years, some of the moons orbiting in Saturn's gravity—along with comets and asteroids—may have begun to smash into each other. As these pieces crashed again and again, they probably broke up into smaller chunks. Eventually, all these chunks and dust would have been pulled by Saturn's gravity into orbit around the planet, forming rings of debris.

Other scientists think that the material that makes up Saturn's rings could have come from one giant collision. Millions of years ago, Saturn may have had an enormous moon that crashed into a comet or another huge space rock. When that happened, rock and ice may have gone flying, eventually creating the rings (and even some of Saturn's smaller moons as well).

The rings around Jupiter, Neptune, and Uranus probably formed in a similar way to the first theory—from collisions between small moons, comets, and asteroids. But Saturn's remain extra spectacular!

RING AROUND THE PLANETS

Compared to Saturn itself, scientists think the rings may be fairly young. What's more, the rings are gradually disappearing. A planet's rings are created by the planet's gravity as it pulls dust and debris into orbit around the planet. This gravity also causes them to vanish. Saturn's gravity is slowly pulling icy particles of the closest rings down into the planet as dust and debris. Eventually, over the course of millions of years, all of the rings could disappear. But there are more rings coming. Scientists think that dust from one of Mars's moons may one day form a new ring around the planet!

SATURN'S NOT-SO-SOLID RINGS

★☆☆
Easy

Through a telescope, Saturn's rings appear so wide and solid that it looks like you could walk on them. You can't though—they're made of pieces of ice and rock that aren't connected at all. Do this experiment to recreate Saturn's rings.

You Need

- Mask or bandanna
- Flashlight
- Table or desk
- Newspaper
- Dark room
- Flour or cornstarch

1. Cover your nose and mouth with the mask or bandanna.

2. Lay the flashlight on its side on a table or desk so that it points at a blank wall.

3. Place the newspaper on the floor between the table that has the flashlight and the wall.

4. Make the room as dark as you can, and then turn on the flashlight. This represents the sun's light.

Tip

Make sure you clean up carefully after this experiment.

5. Stand behind the flashlight so you are looking directly at how the light hits the wall.

6. Toss a small handful of flour or cornstarch into the light to see what happens.

How It Works:

Did the flour look solid for a moment? That's because the specks of flour reflect the light of the flashlight, making them hard to see individually. This activity demonstrates one reason we see Saturn's rings as solid. Saturn's rings are made of individual pieces, too—mostly of ice and rock. Some of these pieces are as small as a grain of salt. Others are bigger than a house. Yet, if you look at Saturn through a telescope, you can't detect these separate pieces. How come? The debris in Saturn's rings reflects sunlight. From far away, this makes it difficult for you to distinguish the individual pieces, and Saturn's rings appear solid. ■

How Do Black Holes Work?

IN SCIENCE FICTION, BLACK HOLES can act as portals to far-off places or even different dimensions. In reality, a *black hole* is a place where gravity is so incredibly strong that nothing can escape its pull—including light.

Black holes can occur in different ways. Scientists think that some black holes, called primordial black holes, formed way back when the universe itself formed. Others, called *supermassive black holes*, might form at the same time that the galaxy they're in forms. These kinds of black holes get their name from their size; they can be up to several billion times as massive as our sun.

Many black holes form from dying stars. If an old star is massive enough, its internal gravity becomes so strong that it can no longer support the weight of the rest of the star. When that happens, the star will explode in a humongous blast called a *supernova*. Sometimes, this supernova leaves behind a black hole.

Once a black hole has formed, its intense gravity will pull matter and light toward it. But sometimes, a disc of swirling matter even forms around the black hole. So where does all this matter in the hole go? Scientists think it forms an incredibly dense center, called a *singularity*.

Illustration of a Black Hole

REAL-LIFE SCIENCE FICTION

Black holes may not be portals to fantastical lands, but according to some theories, they could possibly be used for time travel. The gravity of a black hole is so strong that it warps time itself, making time near the black hole move much slower compared to time elsewhere. Some scientists think that if a spaceship were able to move close enough to a black hole to experience slowed time, it could potentially use this slowed time to travel to the future.

How exactly would this work? Well, say a crew on a spaceship traveled close to a black hole where time moved slowly and stayed for, what felt to them, like a few days. Meanwhile, outside the black hole in the "regular world," time was passing much more quickly—in fact, years were going by! Once the ship moved away from the black hole again—assuming it could escape the black hole's gravitational pull—it would return home to find that years had passed, and it was now the "future."

This all sounds pretty cool but don't rush to buy a ticket on this trip; there'd be no way to go back in time, so this would always be a one-way voyage to the future!

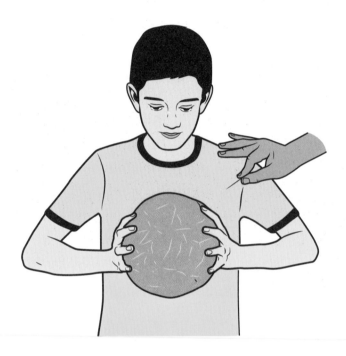

EXPLORE BLACK HOLES

The force of gravity around a black hole is so great that even light can't escape it. Find out how many black holes form and learn more about their pulling power by making these models.

MODEL #1

You Need

- Small round balloon
- Aluminum foil
- Pin or needle

1. Blow up the balloon, and tie it closed.

2. Wrap the balloon in at least four layers of aluminum foil.

3. This is your model star. The balloon is the core (center) of the star, and the aluminum foil layers represent burning gas layers.

4. Gently squeeze the model star. This pressure represents the force of gravity on an active star.

5. Use the pin or needle to pop the balloon (if it hasn't popped already).

6. Squeeze the model star again until it collapses and continue squeezing until the ball of foil is as small as you can make it. This is your black hole.

How It Works:
Normally, the heat made by a star's core provides enough pressure to keep gravity from causing it to collapse. When this is no longer possible, the pressure drops, and the weight of an entire star falls onto the core. The star collapses on itself. If enough matter is left behind, a black hole can form.

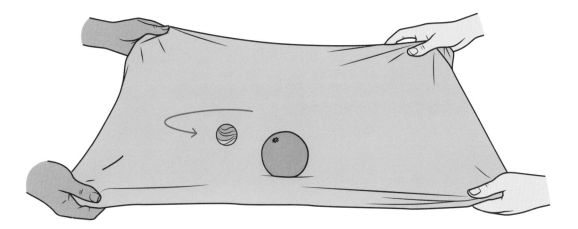

MODEL #2

You Need

- **Stretchy piece of fabric (like a T-shirt that's not made from cotton)**
- **Orange or apple**
- **Marbles**

FOR THREE SCIENTISTS

1. Ask two friends to help you by holding the fabric by its corners and stretching it tightly.

2. Place the fruit in the middle of the fabric. Leaving the fruit in place, put one marble near a corner of the fabric and let it go. Notice what happens.

3. Try to roll the marble across the fabric and observe the shape of its path. Try to roll it faster. Can you roll it quickly enough so that it crosses the fabric so it doesn't get pulled toward the fruit in the middle?

How It Works:
This model shows a black hole's pulling power. The fabric represents space, and the heavy fruit represents a black hole's gravity. Anything traveling too slowly—and too near—will get pulled into it because that force is so strong. If a quickly moving object is far enough away from a black hole, it can get by. ■

How Do Meteor Showers Happen?

METEOROID, METEOR, METEORITE, comet, asteroid—there are lots of things flying through space! So, what's the difference?

A *comet* is a large object—though much smaller than a planet or a moon—made of ice and dust that orbits the sun. If a comet gets too close to the sun, it will start to shed its outer layers as sunlight heats its surface. The ice and dust flowing away from the comet are known as its *tail* and make up a streak that you might see in the sky. This tail is constantly being pushed by sunlight, so it always points away from the sun.

Like a comet, an *asteroid* is also a large object that orbits the sun, but this one is made of rock and metal.

Sometimes, an asteroid or comet will smash into another object. Small pieces that break off and go flying are called *meteoroids*. Every now and then, a meteoroid will enter Earth's atmosphere. When it does, it starts to burn up, leaving a streak behind it—this is called a *meteor*. Most meteors completely burn away as they journey through the atmosphere. But if a meteor survives the atmosphere and lands on Earth, it's known as a *meteorite*!

Sometimes, as Earth travels along its orbit, it will pass through part of a comet's tail or a bunch of meteoroids left behind by an asteroid. This sends tons of meteors into Earth's atmosphere, creating a meteor shower.

WHEN TO SEE METEORS

Thanks to astronomers, we often know when a meteor shower is going to happen ahead of time. This is because there are several groups of debris and meteoroids that Earth regularly passes through during its orbit each year. If you happen to chance upon a clear night when we are passing through one, you may be able to enjoy the show! But it doesn't always happen this way—some meteor showers even take scientists by surprise.

MARSHMALLOW METEORITES

The shooting stars we see blazing across the sky are really meteors. If they hit the ground, they're called meteorites. Create a meteorite model that looks a little like the real thing—and tastes out of this world.

You Need

- Muffin tin
- Paper muffin liners (optional)
- 1 tablespoon butter
- Medium microwavable bowl
- ½ cup chocolate chips
- Small microwavable bowl
- Spoon
- ¼ cup mini marshmallows
- Vanilla wafers, crushed into crumbs
- Knife

1. Line the muffin tin with liners (if you are using them).

2. With an adult's help, use the microwave to melt the butter in the medium bowl. Have the adult help you melt the chocolate chips in the small bowl.

Tip

An easy way to crush the vanilla wafers is to put them in a baggie, close the bag, and press down on them with your hand.

3. Add a spoonful of chocolate to the butter and mix well.

4. Add the mini marshmallows and stir. Keep stirring as you sprinkle in vanilla wafer crumbs. Stop when the mixture has the consistency of cookie dough.

5. Use the spoon to scoop a lump of mixture into the muffin tin.

6. Drizzle some of the remaining chocolate on the top of your meteorite. Use the spoon to spread the chocolate so that the meteorite is completely coated.

7. Let the meteorite cool in the fridge.

8. When it is cool, ask an adult to help you cut it in half, and compare it to the picture below of a real meteorite. Try tasting the meteorite if you'd like! ■

Meteorites

Your tasty marshmallow meteorites are an example of a *chondrite meteorite*. Chondrite meteorites have lumpy outsides, and contain little round structures made of minerals on the inside. They're mostly made of stone. Other meteorites are made almost entirely of nickel and iron.

Did You Know

Earth experiences several regular meteor showers every year. Two of the most famous are the Perseids, which occur in late July or early August, and the Leonids, which fall in November.

How Did Constellations Get Their Names?

HAVE YOU EVER SEEN A LION, a scorpion, or a fish in the sky? If you're familiar with the constellations, you have!

Constellations are groups of stars that seem to form patterns when viewed from Earth. These stars aren't necessarily near one another—in fact, they might be separated by millions and millions of miles. But to us on Earth, they all appear to exist in a flat plane in the sky close to each other, and they continuously show up in the same arrangements, or shapes. Due to Earth's rotation, many of these constellations are only visible at certain times of the year or in certain parts of the world.

Thousands of years ago—at least some 5,500 years before today—people began to imagine that these star patterns looked like familiar shapes. They began to tell stories about these shapes and give them names. Ancient farmers even used the appearance of different constellations throughout the year to keep track of the seasons.

In the ancient Western world, there were at least 48 named constellations. We still use these 48 names today, in addition to 40 more. Many astronomers today recognize 88 constellations, and they usually call them by their Western names, which come from the ancient language of Latin. For example, there's Leo (the lion), Scorpio (the scorpion), and Pisces (the fish). However, many cultures around the world have names for these constellations in their own languages.

Today, we can still see the star groups that our ancient ancestors named—and with our imaginations, we can see the shapes, just like they did!

CONSTELLATION MAPS

Constellation maps can help people keep track of where the different constellations are in relation to each other and to us. How do astronomers make constellation maps? They divide the night sky into the two parts we can see from Earth's Northern Hemisphere (the half above Earth's imaginary middle line, the equator) and from its Southern Hemisphere (the part below).

Next, astronomers need to flatten out what we are

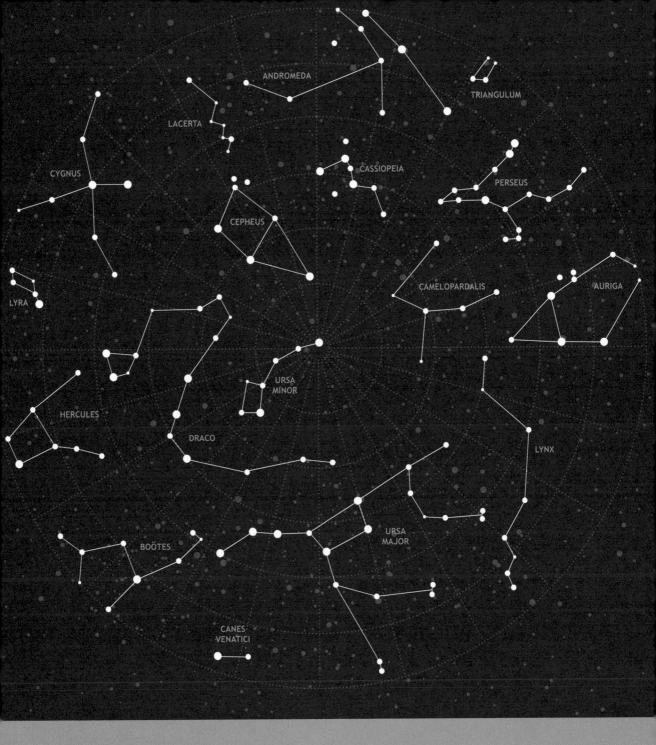

seeing. Imagine the night sky above you as a dome. Now, imagine flattening this dome out into a two-dimensional circle. This is the boundary of a constellation map.

Finally, astronomers divide this two-dimensional circular map into a series of circles and lines that create 88 separate sections. This helps people figure out what constella-

tions they will be able to see in their part of the world at different times of the year.

Easy

CREATE A NEW CONSTELLATION

People have always looked for shapes and patterns in the night sky. You can do the same, day or night!

You Need

- Handful of uncooked lentils, beans, or rice
- Black construction paper
- White chalk, white colored pencil, or white crayon

1. Gently scatter a handful of lentils, beans, or rice across the black piece of paper.

2. Look for a pattern that might represent a picture in these "stars."

3. Circle each star in the pattern using the white chalk, pencil, or crayon.

4. Tip the paper so that the lentils, beans, or rice slide onto your work area. The circles left behind on the paper now represent the stars.

5. Draw lines to connect the stars and create a constellation.

6. Name your constellation and make up a story about it!

Did You Know

The largest constellation is Hydra, the sea serpent.

MAKE A CONSTELLATION PROJECTOR

Turn any ceiling or wall in your house into a piece of the night sky by making your own constellation projector.

You Need

- Small paper cups
- Thin paper
- Pencil or pen
- Scissors
- Glue stick
- Thumbtack or small nail
- Flashlight

1. Place a paper cup bottom-side down on the paper.

2. Trace around the bottom of the cup and then cut out the circle.

3. On the paper circle, redraw the constellations you see here on this page. Draw the dots and lines of the pattern.

4. Glue the paper circle to the bottom of the cup.

5. Carefully use the thumbtack or nail to poke a hole through the cup on each dot.

6. Go into a dark room. Shine a light through the bottom of the cup, with the opening facing the wall.

7. Repeat steps 1–5 with additional cups to create more constellations. ∎

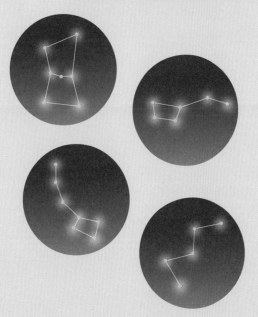

FANTASTIC
FOOD

Quick Challenges

Put a piece of leafy celery in a glass with water and a few drops of food coloring and allow it to sit overnight. See what happens.

Do research to find out what's popular for breakfast in three other countries.

Make a simple salad dressing: Mix six tablespoons of oil with two tablespoons of vinegar, plus a pinch of salt. What happens when you let the mixture sit for a couple of hours?

Invent a new ice-cream flavor.

Has it been a while since you've had a food you don't really like? Try it again! As we get older, our tastes change. You may find a new food that you like.

Write a recipe for how to make your favorite sandwich.

How Do Fizzy Drinks Get Their Bubbles?

***POP, POP, POP!* FIZZY DRINKS** are full of tiny bubbles that constantly float to the surface. These bubbles happen in drinks that have a certain gas, called carbon dioxide, dissolved in them. Some of this gas tries to escape by floating to the top of the liquid and into the air, which forms the bubbles you see and feel on your tongue. The process of dissolving carbon dioxide into a liquid is known as *carbonation*.

Sometimes, carbonation happens naturally in water. This normally happens at a spring where gas bubbles up from the ground into the water. In most drinks though, the carbon dioxide is added.

Scientists make fizzy drinks by pumping carbon dioxide into a container filled with the drink. They make sure to use a lot of pressure when doing this, as this causes a lot of gas to dissolve in the liquid. Then they seal the container to keep the gas in. When you open the drink container—or pour the beverage from a drink dispenser—this gives the gas a place to escape to. Tiny parts of the gas form into the fizzy bubbles and travel up to the surface. That's what gives these drinks their famous *pop!*

RAISIN ELEVATOR

Placing a raisin in a carbonated drink can really give it a lift! See why in this simple experiment.

You Need

- 2 tall, clear drinking glasses, both the same size and shape (tall, thin glasses work best)
- About 3 cups cold seltzer water
- Paper towel
- Marble or glass bead
- Raisin (or dried cranberry)

1. Fill both glasses about three-quarters full with cold seltzer, and put them next to each other.

2. Wipe the marble or glass bead with a paper towel to make sure that it is clean and dust free.

3. Hold the clean marble or glass bead over the top of one glass. Hold the raisin over the top of the other glass.

4. Gently place both the marble or glass bead and the raisin into the seltzer water at the same time.

5. Watch what happens for at least one minute.

How It Works:

The bubbles in fizzy drinks are made of a gas called carbon dioxide. They cling to the raisin's bumps and cracks. Sometimes smaller bubbles stick together and get bigger. If this happens enough times, the raisin floats up. When the raisin reaches the top of the liquid, the bubbles surrounding it pop, and the carbon dioxide mixes with the air above the glass. Without the bubbles, the raisin sinks. More bubbles collect on its surface, and it rises to the top again. The same thing doesn't happen with the marble or glass bead because their surfaces are much smoother than the raisin's, preventing bubbles from clinging to them.

MIX MILK AND COLA

**Both milk and soda can be yummy to drink . . .
but maybe not when mixed together!**

You Need

- 1 small bottle of cola (not diet)
- Funnel
- A few ounces of milk (2% or higher fat content)

Tip

Take a photo of the bottle every 30 minutes to help you compare how the soda looks at different times in the experiment.

1. Remove the label from the bottle of cola.

2. Open the lid of the bottle. Pour out some of the cola so that the bottle is about three-fourths full.

3. Place the bottle in a sink. Use the funnel to carefully add enough milk so that the bottle is full again.

4. Put the lid back on the bottle. (If the mixture is fizzy, wait until the fizzing stops.)

5. Set the bottle in a place where it won't be disturbed for several hours. Observe the results.

How It Works:
Mixing milk and cola causes a chemical reaction. Cola contains phosphoric acid, which makes the milk curdle (form lumps called curds). The curds eventually sink and settle at the bottom of the bottle. ∎

How Do Pumpkins Grow So Big?

THE WORLD'S LARGEST pumpkins can grow to weigh more than 2,500 pounds—that's about as much as a small car! But like most plants, a pumpkin starts out as a seed usually no larger than the tip of your finger.

These seeds are what hold the secret to giant pumpkins. Over many years, gardeners have enjoyed trying to make pumpkins larger and larger. This likely started as a way to feed more people, but eventually, it was just for fun—there are even pumpkin-growing competitions.

To make giant pumpkins, gardeners would select their largest pumpkin, and then plant that pumpkin's seeds. Sometimes, they would breed two different large types of pumpkin together. Over time, this created new varieties of pumpkins designed to grow extra large.

Once they have the right seeds, gardeners plant them in soil. Like most fruits (yes, a pumpkin is a fruit!), pumpkin seeds need soil with lots of nutrients and a lot of water. Vines sprout from these seeds and grow large leaves that help soak up sunlight, which the plant can then turn into energy and sugar (see page 150).

Once tiny pumpkins start to sprout on the vine, gardeners sometimes prune away the smaller ones to give the largest pumpkins more room to grow. Some pumpkins can grow as much as 60 pounds in one day— that's about the weight of a large dog!

PICKING PUMPKINS

There are more than 45 different varieties of pumpkins! These pumpkin types have different qualities that make them good for different things. Pumpkins grown for carving, such as Captain Jack pumpkins and Hobbit pumpkins, tend to be smooth on the sides and flat on the bottom so they can stand up straight. However, they don't taste all that great when cooked. On the other hand, sugar pumpkins or fairytale pumpkins have sweeter flesh and make for great pies.

MAKE PUMPKIN SLIME

Pumpkin pulp is pretty slippery—but you can use this recipe to make some even gooier pumpkin slime.

You Need

- Small or medium whole pumpkin (big enough to fit your hand into once the top is removed)
- Sharp knife
- Spoon
- Medium mixing bowl
- Measuring cup
- ½ cup warm water
- ½ cup clear school glue
- ¼ cup liquid laundry starch

1. Ask an adult to help you remove the top of the pumpkin using a sharp knife. Make sure the hole is big enough for you to fit your entire hand inside.

2. Use the spoon to scrape the sides of the pumpkin to loosen its pulp. Remove about half of the pulp and the seeds. Discard (or see "More Ideas" for how to use the seeds).

3. In a bowl, mix one half cup of water with one half cup of clear school glue. Stir with the spoon.

4. Pour one quarter cup of starch into the pumpkin, and then add in the water and glue mixture.

5. Use your hands to mix it all together!

How It Works:

The glue you added to the pumpkin contains something called a *polymer*. This type of polymer is a substance made of little particles called molecules that are strung together like links on a chain. The starch is a different kind of polymer. It acts like a bridge holding the chains of glue polymer together to make a web of slime. The water in the pumpkin keeps the slime from getting too thick, making it nice and stretchy. ■

More Ideas

Roast your pumpkin's seeds by rinsing away the pulp and patting them dry with a paper towel. Toss the seeds in a little bit of oil and salt, and then spread them out into one layer on a cookie sheet. Ask an adult to help you roast the seeds in the oven at 350°F for 10–15 minutes or until they are golden brown.

Tip

If you want slime that is less sticky, add a little more starch. If you want slime that is less runny, add more glue.

Hard

How Are Fruits Different from Vegetables?

WHEN YOU THINK OF A SAVORY salad with vegetables, you may picture a leafy mixture with cucumbers, tomatoes, and bell peppers. And if you imagine a sweet fruit dessert, rhubarb pie might come to mind. But—surprise!—cucumbers, tomatoes, and bell peppers are actually fruits, and rhubarb is a vegetable. Why do people confuse these two types of food? And what's even the difference between a fruit and a vegetable?

Here's what's going on: When people refer to fruits and vegetables, they usually separate the two by taste; they tend to call sweet-tasting foods that grow in trees and on bushes fruits and savory foods that grow on or in the ground vegetables. But scientists categorize these foods in a different way.

To a *botanist*, or scientist who studies plants, what gets categorized as a fruit depends on whether or not it contains seeds. In botany, fruits are the parts of a plant that contain seeds. Any other part of a plant—from its roots to its leaves to its stem—is called a vegetable. This means that technically, your salads might be full of fruit, and your pie packed with veggies!

BERRY STRANGE

If you think it's odd to find out that so many of the things you think of as vegetables are fruits, get ready for this: Strawberries aren't berries. And neither are raspberries or cranberries! In botany, a berry is categorized as having three layers: an outer skin, a fleshy middle, and a center of seeds. This means that while strawberries and raspberries aren't technically berries, bananas, tomatoes, and kiwis are!

SNEAKY FRUIT

Check out some more surprising fruits!
- Pumpkins
- Olives
- Chilis
- Eggplant
- Corn
- Green beans

CRANBERRY JUICE CODE

Fruits and veggies are full of surprises. Some can be used in really unexpected ways. Check out how you can use cranberry juice to reveal secret messages!

Tip
Wear old clothes for this experiment. Cranberry juice can stain!

You Need

- 2 cups cranberries
- 1 cup water
- Blender or food processor
- Fine mesh strainer or cheesecloth
- Medium bowl
- Rimmed baking sheet or 9-by-13-inch cake pan
- 1 tablespoon baking soda
- ½ cup water
- Spoon
- Cotton swab
- Plain paper
- Hair dryer (optional)

1. Pour the cranberries and one cup of water into the blender. Ask an adult to help you blend them together until they are smooth.

2. Strain the cranberry skins and pulp out of the mixture, collecting the juice in the bowl.

3. Carefully pour a thin layer of the cranberry juice into the pan or baking sheet—just enough to cover the bottom.

4. Mix the baking soda into the half cup of water (it's okay if it doesn't all dissolve).

5. Dip the cotton swab into the water and use it to draw a picture or write a message on the paper. Make sure you use enough!

6. Let the paper dry completely, or carefully use the hair dryer.

7. When you're ready to look at your secret message or drawing, put the paper front side down on top of the cranberry juice.

8. Pat the message gently so that the surface of the paper completely touches the juice. Wait 30 seconds.

9. Turn over the paper to reveal your message!

How It Works:
The cranberry gets its red color from a substance called a *flavonoid*. Flavonoids can change color. They're red when they're in the acidic cranberry but turn purplish blue when mixed with baking soda. So, while most of your paper is stained pink by the cranberry juice, the part that mixes with the baking soda is blue, revealing your message.

RIPEN FRUIT FASTER

Waiting for fruit to get ripe can take some time. See if you can make a green banana ripen faster.

Tip

Bananas turn more yellow when they are ripe. The peel gets softer, and brown spots start to form.

More Ideas

Try this experiment with other fruits. What happens when you put a banana and an orange in the same bag? An orange and an apple?

You Need

- 2 green bananas
- 2 brown paper lunch bags
- 1 apple
- Paper and pencil

1. Put one banana in each bag.

2. Place the apple in one of the bags.

3. Close both bags.

4. Observe both bags every day for one week. Take notes on or draw pictures of what you see.

5. Which banana gets ripe faster?

How It Works:

Fruits like bananas and apples produce a gas called *ethylene* as they start to ripen. The bag with two pieces of fruit in it had more ethylene trapped in it, so that banana ripened more quickly. Not all fruits are like this, though—some, like oranges and grapes, don't continue to ripen after they're picked. ■

How Do Popcorn Kernels Pop?

POPCORN IS NOTHING NEW— in fact, it's been around for at least 6,700 years! Popcorn is a puffed-up (and usually salted and buttered) seed of corn, known as a *kernel*. Normally, a kernel is small and hard. How does it turn into the fluffy, white snack we love?

The dry and tough outside of a kernel is called a *hull*. Inside its hull, each kernel contains starch: a type of nutrient known as a *carbohydrate*. And inside that starch is a bit of moisture in the form of water.

When a kernel of corn gets really hot—perhaps from being cooked over a fire or zapped in a microwave—the water inside it turns into steam. This steam starts to make the starch soft and flexible. It also causes pressure to build up in the kernel! And if you're cooking popcorn in the microwave in a bag, this same steam causes the bag to puff up.

When just enough pressure builds up—*pop!*—the kernel bursts open, releasing both the steam and the now-softened starch. The exploded starch quickly cools, forming the tasty popcorn people know and love. But watch out—if you cook it for too long, all the water will disappear, and the starch will start to burn!

FAILURE TO POP

If you've ever had a bag of popcorn, you've probably come across some hard, un-popped kernels at the bottom of the bag. Some kernels naturally contain less water than others. Without that moisture, heat won't create steam inside the kernel, so the kernel won't pop. Bummer!

PERFECT POPCORN

There are a lot of ways to prepare this delicious snack. Which method makes the fluffiest popcorn?

You Need

- 3 resealable containers with lids, approximately 16 ounces each
- Masking or painter's tape
- Marker or pen
- ¾ cup popcorn kernels
- ¼ cup water
- Rimmed baking sheet
- Colander
- Paper towels
- 1½ teaspoons vegetable oil
- 3 clean brown paper lunch bags
- Microwave-safe plate
- 3 medium or large bowls, all the same size, if possible

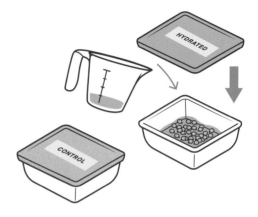

1. Put a piece of tape on the three resealable containers. Label one *control*, one *hydrated,* and the other *dehydrated*. Put one quarter cup of popcorn kernels in each of the three containers.

2. Put the lid on the container labeled *control*. Add one quarter cup of water into the container labeled *hydrated*. Cover the container and let soak for 3 hours.

3. Dehydrate the popcorn kernels from the container labeled *dehydrated*. With help from an adult, heat the oven to 200°F. Spread the popcorn kernals on a baking sheet. Bake for three hours. Let cool, and then put back in the *dehydrated* container and cover it with the lid.

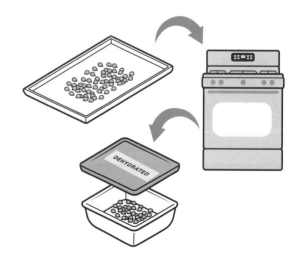

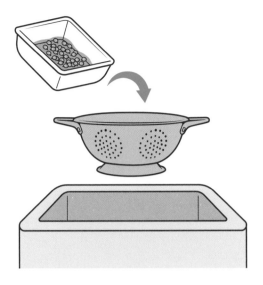

8. Pop the popcorn in the microwave using the popcorn setting, or for 3–5 minutes on high. (Stop the microwave when you can count 2–3 seconds between pops.) Ask an adult to help you remove the plate from the microwave and set this bag aside.

9. Repeat steps 6, 7, and 8 for the hydrated and control kernels, using the appropriate lunch bag for each type.

4. Dump the container of hydrated kernels into a colander over the sink, and let the water drain away. Use paper towels to blot excess water from the kernels and lay them out to dry for approximately 30 minutes.

5. Use the marker to label the paper lunch bags *control, dehydrated,* and *hydrated.*

6. Pour the dried kernels from the container labeled *dehydrated* into the bag labeled *dehydrated.* Add half a teaspoon of oil. Fold the top of the bag over three times, and then shake the bag to coat the kernels with oil.

7. Lay the bag on its side and shake it so that all the kernels settle into one layer. Put this bag on a microwave-safe plate.

10. Dump each bag into a bowl. Put the labeled bag next to each bowl of popcorn so they don't get mixed up.

11. Observe the popcorn in each bowl. Is there a difference in the way it looks? How about its taste? Does one look fluffiest? Did more kernels pop in one bowl than in the other two? ■

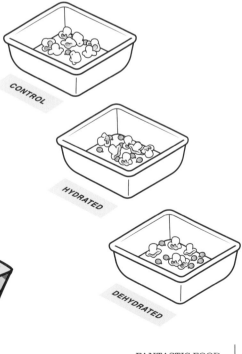

How Do Onions Make Your Eyes Water?

LOTS OF PEOPLE LOVE ONIONS, but not all people love cooking with them. That's because cutting into an onion isn't always pleasant—in fact, it can make your eyes water!

The outside of an onion is wrapped in a papery skin. Beneath that, you'll find the onion's thicker, almost rubbery outer layers. Neither of those on their own are likely to cause you to tear up. But inside the onion, there's something else.

Inside each one of an onion's cells, there is a special substance known as an *enzyme*. An enzyme's usual purpose is to speed up chemical reactions. When someone cuts into an onion, these blobs break open, and the enzymes are free to do their job.

Once released, these enzymes cause some of the other chemicals in the onion to form a new compound called *syn*-propanethial-*S*-oxide. This chemical is so light that it floats through the air, right into contact with the eyes of the person chopping the onion. There, it irritates our sensitive skin, causing our bodies to produce tears to wash the chemical away.

This chemical isn't dangerous, but it can cause an unpleasant burning feeling. For many people, though, the annoyance is worth it for a tasty recipe.

TEAR ATTACK

So why do onions create the chemical *syn*-propanethial-*S*-oxide? In order to make you cry! That's right—onions release this chemical as a defense mechanism. By irritating the animal that is trying to chomp into them, onions have a better chance of avoiding being eaten.

GROW AN ONION GARDEN

You don't need a lot of room to grow onions. Plant some and watch them grow in a juice bottle.

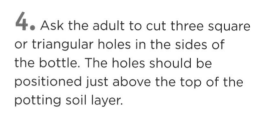

You Need

- Large plastic juice bottle, clean and with label removed
- Scissors
- Handful of small rocks
- Potting soil
- 6–8 small onions (or shallots)
- Duct tape
- Saucer

1. Ask an adult to cut the top off the bottle so it is easier to put your hands inside.

2. Place the small rocks in the bottom of the bottle.

3. Put a layer of potting soil on the rocks that is about as deep as one of your onions is wide.

4. Ask the adult to cut three square or triangular holes in the sides of the bottle. The holes should be positioned just above the top of the potting soil layer.

5. Put three onions inside the bottle with their stem tips pointing out through the holes.

6. Cover the onions with soil.

7. Ask the adult to cut another three holes in the side of the bottle, and then repeat steps 5 and 6. Add as many layers as you can to the bottle—just make sure the onions have enough soil.

8. Ask the adult to cut three more holes in the top part of the bottle so that the last onions can poke out from there.

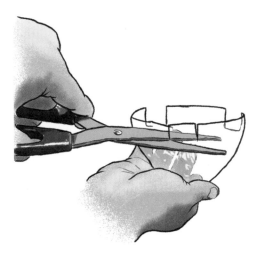

9. Use the duct tape to seal the top back on to the bottle.

10. Carefully add soil through the holes in the top until the last layer of onions is covered.

11. Add some water through the top holes.

12. Put your onion garden on the saucer and place it in a sunny spot. Check on your garden daily and water it when the top of the soil feels dry. Watch it grow!

How It Works:

This experiment wouldn't work with any old fruit or vegetable. Onions and shallots are bulbs. If you could open up the bulb and look inside, you would see a tiny plant. This tiny plant is shielded by parts called scales. The scales not only protect the little plant, but they also store energy that the little plant needs to thrive. Put a bulb in good conditions by giving it water and light, and it's good to grow! ■

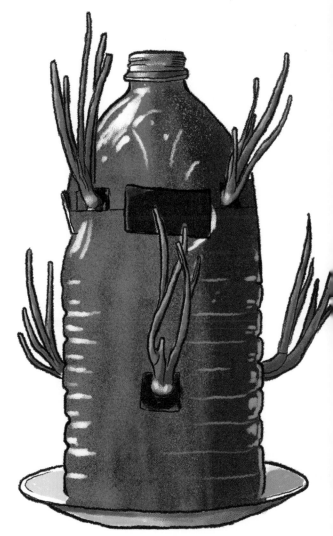

How Do Apples Turn Brown?

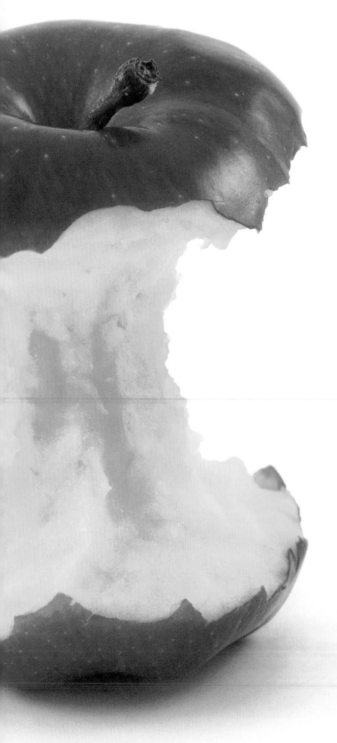

IF YOU'VE EVER LEFT A SLICED apple out for a bit, you've likely noticed that the pieces start to turn a light shade of brown. It may seem odd that the fruit changes color so quickly. But it's perfectly safe to eat. And the process the apple goes through even has a fancy name: *enzymatic browning*.

When an apple is cut or bitten into, oxygen can interact with the flesh of the fruit that is normally hidden under its skin. This flesh contains a substance called an enzyme. When exposed to air, the enzyme begins to interact with the oxygen.

Together, the enzymes and the oxygen begin to make new, harmless chemicals. One of them is called *melanin*. Melanin is the substance, known as pigment, that gives things their color. Melanin is even in your skin and hair! The melanin produced during this interaction between the apple and the air happens to look brown.

Enzymatic browning is very common and can happen to other fruits like pears and bananas. The process is completely harmless, so you can feel free to snack away.

THAT'S BANANAS

Even before their flesh is exposed to oxygen, many fruits start to change colors as they ripen. Many fruits that aren't ripe, such as bananas, apples, tomatoes, and more, start out as green. This is because they contain lots of chlorophyll. *Chlorophyll* helps plants get nutrients, and it also looks green. But in certain fruits, a gas called ethylene starts to go to work as they ripen. This gas breaks down the chlorophyll, leaving behind other chemicals that often look yellow (in fruits like bananas) or red (in fruits like apples or tomatoes). Ethylene also starts to make the fruit softer and more flavorful— and ready to be eaten.

FRESH APPLES

A sliced apple that's been left out will start to brown. Is there a way to keep it fresh looking? Do this experiment to find out.

You Need

- 5 small plastic zipper bags
- Permanent marker
- ¼ cup bottled lemon juice
- ¼ cup white vinegar
- ¼ cup skim milk
- ¼ cup honey
- 1 apple
- Sharp knife
- Stopwatch

1. Use the marker to label the bags *lemon, vinegar, milk, honey,* and *control.*

2. Dump the lemon juice, vinegar, milk, and honey into the correctly labeled bags. Do not put anything into the bag labeled *control.*

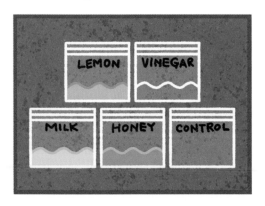

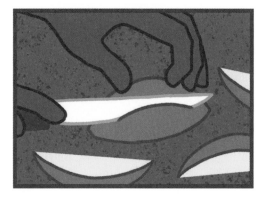

3. Ask an adult to cut five apple slices that are all about the same size.

4. Put one slice of apple into each bag. Seal the bags and shake each one to coat the apple slice in the liquid.

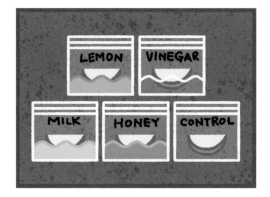

5. Wait for three minutes, and then dump any extra liquid out of the bags and into the sink.

6. Record what the apple slices look like using words or pictures. Wait 10 minutes and record what they look like again. Do you see a difference?

How It Works:
Due to the process of enzymatic browning, the inside of an apple turns brown when it comes into contact with the air (see pages 264–265). Lemon juice and vinegar have acids in them that keep this process from happening. Honey has a different kind of molecule in it that keeps the apple from turning brown. Milk doesn't have an acid, or any other molecule in it to keep the apple from turning brown. ∎

How Is Rock Candy Made?

ROCK CANDY MIGHT BE ONE OF the simplest kinds of candy—after all, it's made from water and sugar. But this candy also has a trick that's not so simple: It grows itself!

To make rock candy, you start by dissolving sugar into hot water—lots and lots of sugar. Sugar dissolves into water because the tiny parts—or *molecules*—of the water break up the molecules of the sugar. This process happens quickly when the water is hot, as heat makes the molecules work faster.

For rock candy, so much sugar has to be dissolved into the water that it creates a saturated solution. A *saturated solution* is the name for when the maximum amount of one substance has been dissolved into another. This means that absolutely no more sugar could be dissolved into the hot water.

Because of how fast its molecules move, hot water can hold more dissolved sugar than cool water. But when the saturated solution starts to cool, it won't be able to hold as much dissolved sugar. That sugar will have to find somewhere to go.

When you leave a string or a wooden skewer in the saturated solution, that is where the extra sugar will head. As the solution cools and evaporates, and molecules of sugar start to form solids again, they will cling to each other and to the string or skewer. This forms sugar crystals. As evaporation continues over time, these sugar crystals will attract more sugar, and more crystals will grow until your string or stick is covered in hardened sugar—rock candy.

MAKE ROCK CANDY

Cook up some sugar and crystallize a sparkly treat.

Safety Tip

Boiling water and sugar can cause burns. Have an adult help you with steps 3 and 4.

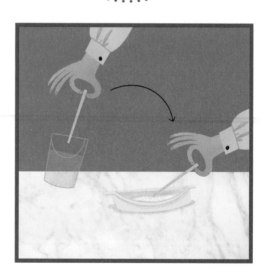

1. Pour a few tablespoons of sugar onto a plate. Dip the end of each skewer into water. Roll the end of the wet skewer in sugar. Coat only the bottom inch or two. Set the skewers aside to dry on a wire rack.

2. Fill the jars with hot water and set aside.

3. Working with an adult, boil one cup of water in a saucepan. Add one cup of sugar. Stir slowly and carefully. (Splashes can burn!) Once the sugar dissolves, add the second

cup of sugar and stir again. Bring to a boil, and simmer for a minute or two. Remove the pan from heat, and let it cool for 20–30 minutes. The liquid should still be warm.

4. Empty the water out of the jars. Add a few drops of food coloring and flavoring to each jar if you want. Have an adult pour the warm sugar solution into each jar. If you need to, stir to combine.

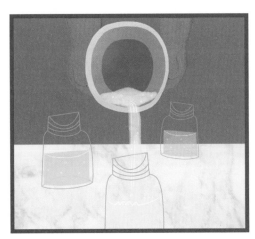

5. Attach a clothespin to the top of each skewer. Balance the clothespins on the tops of the jars. The skewers should hang straight down with the sugared end of each skewer about a half inch above the bottom of the

jar. Tape the clothespins and skewers in place if they are wiggly.

6. Place the jars in a safe spot that doesn't get hot or sunny. Wait 5–14 days, or until rock candy forms on the end of the skewer. Break the crust at the top of the jar, pour out the extra liquid, and remove the candy. You may need to set the jar in hot water to warm it up before you can pull the candy out.

How It Works:
Warm water can dissolve more sugar than cool water can. By starting with boiling water, you can make a sugar solution that is very, very concentrated. As it cools off, the particles of sugar in it start to stick together and form crystals. ■

How Does Eating Mint-Flavored Things Make You Feel Cold?

MINT AND MINT-FLAVORED FOODS are famous for being cool, refreshing, and crisp. But unlike other chilly snacks and beverages—such as ice cream or cold drinks—mint isn't cold to the touch. In fact, if you hold a mint leaf or a piece of mint-flavored gum in your hand, it will probably feel room temperature. Yet once you put it into your mouth, your mouth might start to tingle or go numb. Why is that?

All over your body—including inside your mouth—you have cells that are designed to send messages to your brain. These cells can send messages about how hot or cold something is, what it tastes like, what it feels like, and more. But when these cells come into contact with a certain chemical found in mint, they get confused.

Although mint isn't actually chilly itself, it contains a chemical that tricks your mouth into feeling cold. This chemical is called *menthol*. When your cells encounter menthol, they react the same way that they might if you were to touch an ice cube or something else chilly—by sending signals to your brain that you are touching something cold! This means that when you chew on mint and release the menthol inside, your brain interprets this menthol as chilly. *Brrr!*

FEEL THE BURN

When you eat something minty, you are not actually eating something cold. Similarly, when you chew on something spicy, you're not necessarily chewing on something hot in temperature—but it still burns! This is because spicy foods contain a special chemical just like mint contains menthol. This chemical, called *capsaicin*, tricks your brain into thinking you're eating something hot.

SWEET SPARKS

Some mints can do more than just make our mouths feel cool—they can make some pretty cool-looking sparks, too!

- Dark room
- Hard-candy mints flavored with wintergreen oil
- Mirror
- Pliers (optional)

3. Hold the mirror in front of your face.

4. Bite down on the candy and chew a few times with your mouth open.

1. Ask permission from an adult before doing this experiment. If they say it's okay for you to do the activity, enter the dark room. Count to 100 slowly, to give your eyes time to get used to the dark.

2. Put a wintergreen candy between your molars (back teeth) so that you can bite down on its outside edge.

How It Works:
The sugar in the mint candy is made up of tiny crystals. When these crystals are put under pressure and crushed, they make a tiny spark. Wintergreen mints are flavored with an oil that makes some of the light, called ultraviolet (UV) light, visible. ∎

Did You Know?

Some scientists have found that the smell of peppermint can help wake you up if you're feeling sleepy.

Safety Tip

If you have braces or sensitive teeth, or if you don't like the taste of mint, use pliers to break the candy instead of your teeth.

FUN AND GAMES

Quick Challenges

Grab a deck of cards and practice learning how to shuffle them.

Make a stack of blocks on a smooth tablecloth or piece of paper. See if you can pull the tablecloth quickly out from under the blocks.

Teach a friend or family member how to play your favorite game.

Make shadow shapes using your hands.

Draw a maze and ask another person to solve it.

Make up your own game of hopscotch. Use chalk to draw the board on the ground outside.

How Do Parachutes Open and Float?

ONE SECOND, A PARACHUTE IS folded up inside a pack on a person's back, and the next, it's fluttering through the air, letting the person float gently to the ground. How is it that parachutes slow a person's descent to the ground—and how do they open correctly?

The first step of getting a parachute to work is packing it correctly so that the opening is at the bottom. This means that the top of the parachute (the part shaped like an umbrella or the top of a balloon) comes out of the pack first.

At the very top of a parachute is a much smaller miniature parachute, called a *pilot chute.* When the person pulls a release cord, the pack opens, and the pilot chute comes out. When this pilot chute catches the air, it is pulled upward, dragging the rest of the parachute out of the pack as well.

As the person is falling through the air, air rushes up into the parachute from the bottom. This upward push of air acts against the gravity of the falling person, pushing up on the parachute and slowing the person down. Now, thanks to the balance between gravity and the upward push of air, the person can safely float to the ground.

PARACHUTE CHALLENGE

Make a parachute out of household materials to help guide a weight safely to the ground.

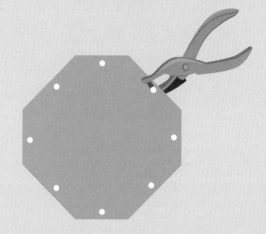

1. Use the scissors to cut a square from your plastic bag or fabric.

2. Cut off the four corners of the square to make an octagon.

3. Use the hole punch to make a hole in the middle of each side for a total of eight holes.

4. Thread one piece of string through a hole. Gently tie and tape it in place. Repeat for the other holes.

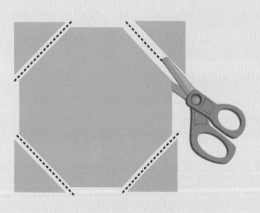

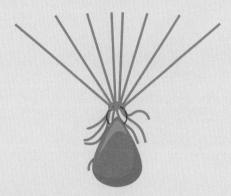

5. Tie the other ends of each string to the weight.

6. Test your parachute: Drop the parachute while standing on a sturdy stool or chair. (Have someone hold the stool or chair while you're standing on it.) Did your weight land gently? If not, try again!

How It Works:
Objects fall to the ground because of the force of gravity. The air pushes up against the object while it is falling, but it's not enough to slow the object down and prevent it from hitting the ground with a crash. A parachute's wide canopy gives the air something to push up on, slowing the object's fall. ■

More Ideas

Try to make a parachute for a lighter weight . . . and a heavier one! Find out what happens when you punch a small hole in the middle of the parachute.

How Do Fireworks Explode?

HISTORIANS THINK THE FIRST-EVER fireworks were created about 2,000 years ago in China, when people tossed bamboo sticks onto a fire and they exploded. Bamboo has segments that contain water and other substances. When the bamboo is heated, these materials also get hot and vaporize or convert to a gas. With continued heating, the gas trapped in the bamboo compartment expands, and eventually the bamboo compartment violently explodes, creating a loud noise.

According to legend, Chinese scientists trying to make a potion for immortality accidentally invented an explosive powder around the year 800. This powder—a blend of different chemicals and substances—is still used in fireworks today. People who make fireworks shape the powder, sometimes called black powder, into hard pellets known as *stars*. They also mix in different chemicals and metals. Firework designers put these stars into containers called *shells*.

Then, extra black powder is packed into another part of the shell. This powder is ignited, or set on fire—and it explodes! However, this explosion is controlled through a fuse so that the firework does just what it's meant to. When the powder explodes, hot air pushes against the ground, shooting the firework into the sky.

Meanwhile, the fuse keeps burning. The designers time it so that right about when the firework is as high as it will go, the burning fuse reaches the stars, and a second explosion happens. This explosion is much larger and—thanks to the metal and chemicals in the stars and how the stars are arranged in the shell—creates amazing colors and shapes, going out with a bang.

GOING OUT *WITHOUT* A BANG

Not only do the people who make fireworks design them to have certain shapes and colors, they also design them to explode with certain sounds. This is why some fireworks sizzle, others crackle, and some even whistle. Some people are even designing quiet fireworks so that pets and people nearby who hear them won't be startled.

FIREWORKS IN A GLASS

Reds, blues, yellows, and greens—fireworks light up the sky during celebrations. You can't make your own fireworks, but you can reproduce their cool colors and shapes in this activity.

1. Fill the glass about three-fourths full with warm water.

2. Fill the small bowl with oil. Put 5–6 drops of food coloring into the oil. Observe what happens.

3. Use the fork to stir the oil until the food coloring is broken into small drops.

4. Pour the oil slowly into the glass of water. Watch and observe what happens.

How It Works:

Food coloring is mostly water, and water and oil don't mix. Instead of dissolving in the oil, the food coloring stayed in droplets, even when you stirred them. When you poured the oil and food coloring into the warm water, the oil started to float. That's because oil is less dense than water. It didn't just float on the warm water in the glass . . . it also floated on the watery food coloring, pushing those droplets to the bottom. Once the food coloring droplets touched the water, though, they fell apart, making firework-like patterns as they fell to the bottom of the glass. ■

Did You Know?

Fireworks make use of substances that have sodium, copper, and other metals that burn different colors after they are launched into the sky. Sodium, a major part of salt, burns yellow when exposed to heat. Copper burns bluish green, and lithium mixed with other chemicals makes a reddish color when it burns.

How Are Crayons Made?

BEFORE CRAYONS EXISTED, people still drew pictures—even 70,000 years ago! Back then, our ancestors had to use *pigments*, or colors, that they found in nature. This could have been from berries, charcoal, colored clay, or *chalk*— which is the soft, ground-up form of a rock called limestone.

Later, artists began shaping chalk into sticks and adding color—like we still do today. But it wasn't until the early 1900s that crayons were invented. Crayons are a mix of pigment and wax.

First, the wax is melted down until it becomes a liquid. Then, different pigments are added to get different colors. After that, the colorful wax is poured into different molds. These molds shape the wax. They are often shaped like long, pointed tubes, but can also come in fun shapes and different sizes.

Next, the wax needs to cool. To hurry this process along, lots of factories pour cold water around the molds. Then the extra wax is scraped away, and the crayons are taken out of their tubes.

To wrap up, people inspect the crayons to make sure they look right, and often add paper labels. Now the crayons are done being created and are ready to help *you* create art!

What are some of your favorite crayon colors? There are so many—people love to find new pigments and create new shades of colors. But whenever there's a new color, someone needs to give it a new name. This happens in several ways. Sometimes, people working at a crayon company submit ideas or name new colors. Other times, companies hold competitions to pick the best name for a new shade. Some crayon companies even use official color dictionaries. The names can get, well, pretty colorful!

MAKE A CRAYON CANDLE

Don't throw out old or broken crayons. Use them to make a brightly colored candle instead.

You Need

- Pieces of an old candle, wick removed
- 5-ounce paper cups
- Scissors
- Candle wick
- Oven mitt
- Toothpicks
- Small jar or juice glass
- Old crayons (about one whole crayon for each colored layer)

1. Put the wax pieces from the old candle into a cup. Cut a piece of wick that is a little bit taller than the jar or glass with the scissors.

2. Put the wax in the microwave for one minute. Carefully remove the cup from the microwave using the oven mitt. Use a toothpick to stir the wax. Put the cup back into the microwave and heat for 30 seconds. Take it out and stir it. Repeat this step until the wax is completely melted.

3. Pour a thin layer of wax into the jar or glass. Put the piece of wick into the jar or glass so that its bottom is covered by the wax. Let the wax cool and harden. Hold the wick in place until the wax cools and hardens.

4. Choose the color you want for the bottom layer. Gather crayon pieces of that color and peel the paper from them. Put the crayon pieces into a cup. Put the cup in the microwave for two minutes. Stir with a toothpick, and heat for 30 seconds at a time until the crayons are completely melted.

the jar or glass over the wax. Let cool completely, at least 30 minutes.

6. Repeat the melting process for the next layer. Continue until the jar or glass is completely full. Trim the wick with the scissors and your candle is complete! ■

5. Let cool for 30 seconds, and then pour the melted crayon layer into

Safety Tip

Ask an adult for help with anything hot or sharp.

Tip

If you can't find wicks in a store, you can make your own by coating a piece of cotton string in melted candle wax.

How Does a Moving Bike Stay Upright?

TRY TO BALANCE ON A BICYCLE that isn't moving, and the bike is likely to flop to one side. But start pedaling, and the bike stays up! But how?

The truth is, scientists don't know! Scientists used to think that bicycles balanced thanks to something called *gyroscopic motion*. Gyroscopic motion means that a rotating object—such as a bicycle wheel—tends to want to continue rotating in the same direction and at the same angles. For example, if you are moving forward on a bicycle and lean to the side slightly, the bicycle is likely to shift direction and correct itself to stay upright.

However, scientists have recently learned that there is a lot more to it than that. In fact, they are still working to understand the exact combination of things that keeps a bike balanced and moving upright.

That being said, scientists have discovered that there might be something much more important than gyroscopic motion when it comes to keeping a bike upright: your brain. When you are in motion, your brain and body work together constantly to keep you balanced.

BICYCLES FROM BEFORE

Just because your brain might be the main reason you stay upright on a moving bicycle, that doesn't mean that a bike's design is unimportant. In fact, today's bicycles are engineered to be easier, safer, and faster than ever before. In the past, some of the first wooden and iron bicycles were super uncomfortable, thanks to the fact that they didn't absorb any shock. Later bicycles that had one giant front wheel and a small back wheel were more comfortable but dangerous, as the rider could fall from a greater height. Eventually, bicycles were improved with more comfortable seats, more cushioned tires, and better proportions . . . and they just keep getting better!

This includes making tons of tiny adjustments as you walk or run. The same thing goes for when you ride a bike!

When you are on a bicycle, your brain is constantly correcting your motions to keep you moving and balanced—even if you don't notice it. So, it may not be the design of the bicycle that keeps it upright, but the design of your mind.

EGG HELMET

Helmets are an important part of riding a bike safely. See how by trying to keep an egg from breaking.

You Need

- 2 raw eggs
- 2 plastic zipper bags
- Flat stone or brick (or sidewalk)
- Foam, towels, blankets, or bubble wrap for padding
- Bucket or box
- Low stool or chair
- Measuring tape

1. Put a raw egg inside a plastic bag. Seal the bag. This egg represents a bicycle rider's head.

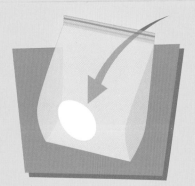

2. Drop the bag onto the stone or other hard surface from a height of one foot. Check to see if the egg cracked or broke.

3. Place the second raw egg into a plastic bag. Seal the bag.

4. Put about six inches of padding in the bottom of the box or bucket. This padding represents a bike helmet.

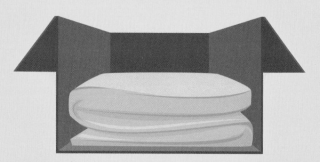

5. Stand on a sturdy stool or chair (for extra support, have someone hold the stool or chair) and hold the bag four feet above the box. Drop the bag, and then check the egg to see if it cracked.

How it Works:

When dropped, objects (like eggs) hit the ground with a certain amount of force. Isaac Newton discovered that for every force there is another force that is equal but in the opposite direction. So, the ground is pushing upward on the egg with the same amount of force as the egg is pushing downward on the ground. If the upward-pushing force of the ground is strong enough, the egg will crack. The padding absorbs a lot of the downward force of the egg. It doesn't push up on the egg as hard, so the eggshell stays whole. ◼

More Ideas

Try different materials to catch the egg. Which allows you to drop the egg from the highest height without cracking? What happens if you drop the egg from a low height but wrap it in padding first?

Did You Know

People have been wearing bicycle helmets for a little over 100 years, and the first bicycle helmet law was passed in California in the late 1980s.

How Do Bubbles Form?

IF YOU'VE EVER TAKEN A BATH, you know that bubbles can form naturally in water. Like all things, water is made up of tiny parts called *molecules*. The molecules in water tend to like to stick to each other. When water mixes with air—such as when a bathtub is being filled—the air can get trapped in pockets of "sticky" water, forming bubbles. (This is also what happens if you use a straw to blow bubbles in a glass of water.)

However, bubbles made from just water and air usually pop very quickly. This is due to something called *surface tension*. Tension is the amount of strain or force acting on an object. Some shapes— like a sphere, or a bubble shape—can decrease the tension on an object's surface. This is why bubbles naturally form into round shapes: It makes them stronger. Even so, water has such a high surface tension that— *pop!*—even a round bubble will burst.

However, when you add soap to the water, something else happens.

The molecules of the soap mix with the water. This dilutes the water, increasing the distance between water molecules. This lowers the surface tension, making a mixture that is much more flexible. Thanks to soap, the bubbles in a bubble bath stick around a lot longer and even form more easily.

This is also true for the bubbles you blow from a wand. When you gently blow against a film of the soapy mixture, the air pushes against the film. However, thanks to the soap molecules, the mixture stretches instead of breaking. When you stop blowing, the molecules draw back together, trapping the air inside. A bubble is born!

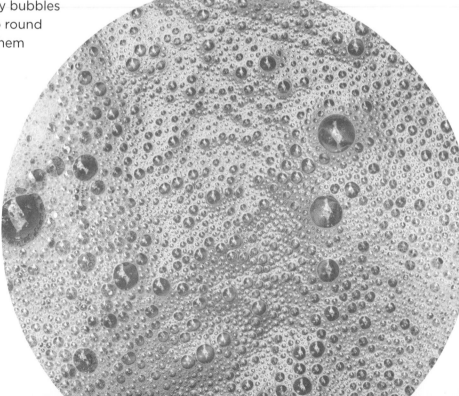

EXPERIMENT WITH BUBBLES

Make your own bubble solution, and then do some amazing bubble experiments!

BUBBLE SOLUTION

You Need

- 6 cups distilled water
- 1 tablespoon glycerin or corn syrup
- ½ cup blue liquid dish soap
- Large tub or bucket

1. Mix all the ingredients in a large tub or bucket.

SQUARE BUBBLES

You Need

- Plastic drinking straws
- Modeling clay or dough
- Bubble solution
- Bubble wand

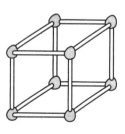

2. Dip the cube into the bubble solution until it is completely covered, and then lift it out.

3. Dip the bubble wand into the solution. Blow a bubble and let it drop into the top of the cube. Watch a square bubble form inside the cube.

1. Cut six drinking straws in half. Use these pieces and the modeling clay or dough to build a cube.

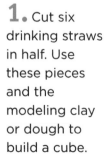

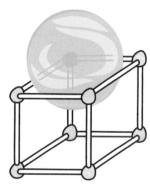

SKATING BALLOON

You Need

- Bubble solution
- Glass pie plate
- Bubble wand
- Small round balloon, inflated and tied

1. Pour just enough bubble solution into the pie plate to cover the bottom.

2. Use the bubble wand to blow a small bubble and let it drop onto the layer of solution. It will probably become a half-bubble, which is okay.

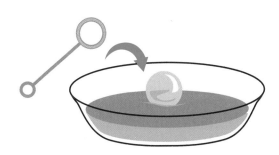

3. Rub the balloon on your hair for about 30 seconds.

4. Hold the balloon close to the bubble, and then slowly pull the balloon away. The bubble should follow the balloon around the pie plate.

How It Works:
Rubbing your hair and the balloon together builds up a static charge on the balloon (see the lightning experiment on pages 162–163). This charge attracts, or pulls on, the opposite charges that are drawn onto the soap bubble. ■

How Do Lava Lamps Work?

IMAGINE A LAMP LIT BY THE GLOW of molten lava. Of course, lava lamps don't actually contain lava—but they do sort of look like it.

Invented in the 1960s, lava lamps are lamps built into clear containers full of a mysterious, colorful goo that seems to ooze and move on its own. In reality, this substance is not so mysterious—it's wax!

Most lava lamps contain a mixture of a type of wax and a liquid, usually water or oil. The wax is often brightly colored, and the liquid can be colorful or clear. So why don't the two colorful substances mix together to form one big, gloopy mess? This is thanks to the different molecules that make up each substance.

Unlike some molecules, which stick together, the molecules that make up both the lava lamp's wax and its liquid do not. No matter how long they are in the same container, the liquid and wax will not merge. This is known as being *insoluble*. Some versions of lava lamps are made from other combinations of materials that are insoluble, like water and oil.

As for the movement of the "bubbles"—that's where the lamp at the bottom of the container comes in. When the lamp is off, the wax is cool and in a solid state. When it is solid, the wax is denser than water. Density refers to how compact a substance is—its mass, or matter, relative to the space it occupies. Because solid wax is denser than the lamp's liquid, it sits at the bottom of the lamp.

However, when the lamp is turned on, it gets hot. This melts the wax. The liquid wax has a lower density than the other liquid in the lamp. Because of this, the liquid wax now rises to the top of the lamp. Once it gets there, it starts to cool down, getting denser and denser until it falls back to the bottom of the lamp and the cycle starts again.

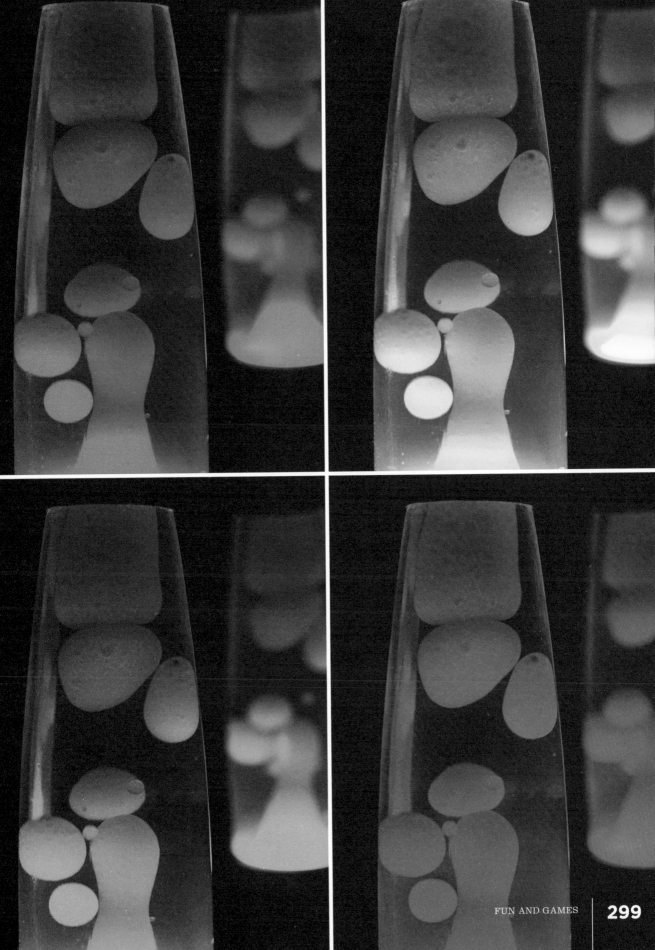

LAVA LAMP

Make your own "lava lamp"—minus the wax and heat!—and watch these colorful blobs erupt and float.

You Need

- Plastic cover or old vinyl tablecloth, to protect your work area
- Baking soda
- Clear glass jar or bottle (tall and narrow works best)
- Cooking oil (canola oil works best)
- Small bowl
- White vinegar
- Food coloring
- Spoon
- Flashlight or cell phone with light
- Small plastic zipper bag (large enough to hold a cell phone)

1. Spread out the plastic cover or tablecloth. Place two or three spoonfuls of baking soda in the container.

2. Pour the oil into the container until it is about two-thirds full. Don't stir or shake the container; you want the baking soda to remain at the bottom for now.

3. Pour vinegar into the small bowl and add four drops of food coloring.

Safety Tip

Do not put a lid on the bottle or jar. Do not pour the liquid down the drain because it could cause a clog. Ask an adult to help you dispose of it safely.

6. Turn out the room lights and enjoy! The chemical reaction will only last for a short while.

4. Slowly spoon the colored vinegar into the container. Bubbling blobs of color will move through the oil.

5. If using a cell phone light, turn it on and carefully seal the phone in the plastic bag. Place the container on the phone light. If using a flashlight, hold the flashlight under or behind the container.

How It Works:
When an acid (vinegar, which contains acetic acid) comes in contact with a base (baking soda, also known as sodium bicarbonate), a chemical reaction occurs that results in carbon dioxide and water. When carbon dioxide (a gas) is in a liquid, bubbles form. Here, because the bubbles of carbon dioxide are coated in food coloring, we can see the colored bubbles rise to the top and "pop." Why does the vinegar sink down to the bottom of the container? The vinegar is denser than the oil. ∎

Did You Know?

A town named Soap Lake, Washington, once attempted to build a 60-foot-tall lava lamp. A lamp this size would hold over 100,000 gallons of liquid! The town has decided to build a digital lava lamp instead.

How Do Roller Coasters Make Riders Feel Weightless?

AS YOU STRAP INTO A ROLLER coaster, you are being secured very safely in one place. However, there will still be a lot happening to your body during the ride, even as you yourself remain fairly still.

Most roller coasters are designed to go fast—very fast! The sudden speed, or *acceleration*, of a coaster causes gravity to push back against your body. On top of that, the ride probably includes lots of sudden turns, jolts, and even upside-down loops that add to this pressure.

But sometimes, such as when the coaster gets to the top of a hill or takes a sudden drop, riders will feel as though all that gravity went away in an instant. In these moments, the force of acceleration equals the force of gravity, so the two balance out. The pressure is suddenly gone, leading to a weightless feeling. But that doesn't mean every part of you is staying still; you are still moving on the *inside*.

Scientists found that your internal organs actually move slightly during roller-coaster rides. It's completely harmless but can help create that funny free-fall feeling. *Wheee!*

THE SCIENCE OF SCARY

Roller coasters can be super scary—after all, you're shooting forward at top speeds, often at great heights and sometimes upside down. So why do so many people love them? According to scientists, it can be fun for humans to feel scared when we are in safe situations. This lets us play out scenarios that might otherwise be dangerous without any of the risk. In these situations, our brains create certain chemicals that make us feel alert, excited, and happy.

BUILD A ROLLER COASTER

Build your own roller coaster right at home and watch it in action!

Tip

Make sure the end of your roller coaster track isn't pointed at a window!

You Need

- At least 6 feet of 1½-inch diameter foam pipe insulation
- Box cutter or scissors
- Masking or duct tape
- High stool, chair, desk, or table
- Glass marbles or ball bearings small enough to fit through the insulation

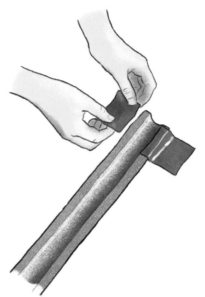

1. Ask an adult to use the box cutter or scissors to cut the pipe insulation in half from top to bottom.

2. Bend one end of the insulation pieces into a loop.

3. Use the tape to attach the loop to the floor. Put at least one piece of tape on either side of the loop. Important: Make sure the tape doesn't block the channel in the insulation.

Tip

Cut several three- to four-inch strips of masking or duct tape before you begin.

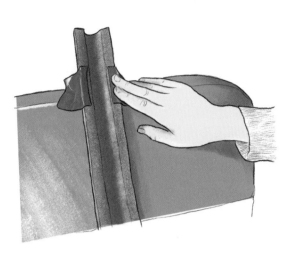

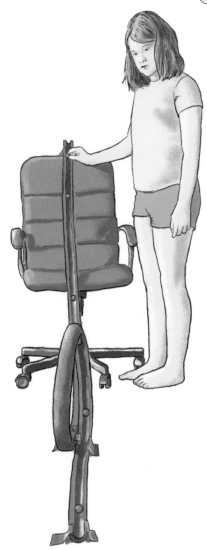

4. Use tape to attach the other end of the insulation to a high stool, table, chair, or desk. Make sure there are no crimps or folds in the insulation.

5. Put the marble or ball bearing at the top of the loop. Let go of the marble to see if it rolls the whole way around the loop. If it doesn't, adjust the ends of your track until it works. ■

Did You Know?

One of the first roller coasters in the United States also had a "real" job to do—it carried coal. Miners would fill the "cars" with coal, and let gravity carry them down the hill. Eventually, people paid for a ride in the car just for fun.

More Ideas

Use more insulation to add more track to your roller coaster. Roll more than one marble or ball bearing down the track at once.

MAKING A
DIFFERENCE

Quick
Challenges

Instead of getting rid of an old pair of socks, turn them into arm warmers! Use scissors to cut off the toe area. This is for your fingers. Then cut a small slit into the heel for your thumb.

Make signs to hang beneath light switches in your house to remind yourself and others to turn off the lights when they're not in use.

Time yourself in the shower. Make your next one two minutes shorter. (But don't skip washing anything!)

Research and make a list of what kinds of items you can and can't recycle in your area.

Learn about a plant that is native to your area, and plant one.

Think of one way you can use less plastic.

How Do Community Gardens Work?

WORKING IN A GARDEN CAN HELP lower a person's stress and increase their happiness. Plus, the garden provides much-needed food for insects, especially pollinating animals like bees and some flies. And, of course, it can grow delicious food and beautiful flowers!

But gardens can also take up lots of space, which can be hard for people to come by. Luckily, there are community gardens: plots of land shared by many members of a community. Sometimes, a local organization or group of people may rent or buy a plot of land from the city or individual landowners. People can sign up to grow sections of the garden, or volunteers can donate their time to help tend the plants.

On top of the natural benefits of a garden, community gardens can bring greenery and food to areas where food isn't normally grown and healthy food options are limited. These places are known as *food deserts*. Community gardens are also wonderful ways for people to connect and get to know their neighbors.

BUILD A COMMUNITY GARDEN

A lot of planning takes place before any plants go in the ground in a community garden.

You Need

- A lot of planning
- Gardening tools
- Building supplies
- Seeds
- Soil
- Water

1. Ask one or more adults to help you with this project. Then, find out what kind of garden your community wants: With an adult's help, create a survey about the garden and send it out to people in your community. Collect feedback. Hold a meeting to discuss the results and start making important decisions.

2. Based on the feedback you receive, decide which kind of community garden you want to have. Will everyone have their own plot? Will everyone work as a team on one large garden? Will you keep, sell, or donate the food you grow?

3. Consider finding a sponsor. If you're starting from scratch, a sponsor, like a local business, can help pay for the supplies and tools you'll need to create your garden. With the help of a grown-up, call or email potential sponsors to let them know about your project. Ask if they would be interested in partnering with you.

4. Have an adult help you choose a site. Gardens need healthy soil, at least six hours of sunshine a day, and a dependable water source. Get permission and any necessary permits from your community leaders to create the garden in your selected site.

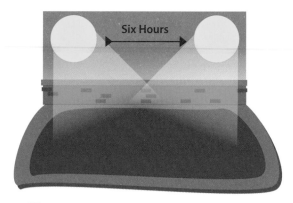
Six Hours

5. Establish the rules. Create a work schedule. Identify work hours and days. Determine, in detail, how you will assign plots, manage weeds and pests, store and share tools, etc. Decide whether you will charge dues. Things will run much more smoothly if everyone agrees on the ground rules from the beginning.

6. Make a plan. Measure the site and draw your plan. Include the length and width of each plant bed. Don't forget to include space for aisles so people can walk between the beds in the garden. You might also want to build a fence around your garden to protect it.

7. Plant the garden. Plan a community workday to clear the land, prepare the soil, and get the plants in the ground. ■

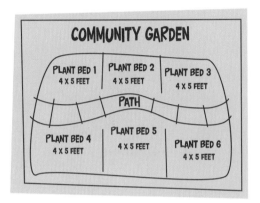

Tip

Make a sign that welcomes gardeners but that also tells the story of why your community came together to create the garden. You could also list the garden's rules at the entrance. These signs tell newcomers and visitors how special your space is.

How Can We Protect Animals Like Bees?

EVEN SMALL ANIMALS CAN IMPACT the world in huge ways. Take bees, for example. There are many different kinds of bees, from metallic sweat bees that are smaller than your pinkie nail to hairy, orange bumblebees that are as big as your thumb. The role these little animals play in your life is enormous: Bees are responsible for keeping many plants—including many of the ones we eat for food—growing and reproducing.

This is because most bees are great pollinators. *Pollinators* are animals that take pollen from one plant and bring it to another. Pollen is necessary for plants to make fruits and seeds and to create new plants. Some plants rely on the wind to carry their pollen, but most rely on pollinators.In fact, at least 75% of plants benefit from pollinators!

These plants are an important part of a healthy planet. And many people need these plants for food, medicine, materials, and more. In fact, some scientists say that bees are responsible for pollinating the plants that provide about one out of every three bites of food you take. But bees aren't the only pollinators: Other animals—like bats, birds, butterflies, and beetles—are pollinators, too.

Today, many pollinators are endangered. Climate change and human activities are damaging places where pollinators live. Chemicals that people use in their lawns or on farms, called *pesticides*, can also be harmful to these animals. But people are fighting to protect pollinators.

Leaders and scientists across the world are finding ways to cut back on pesticides and to study ways to keep pollinators healthy. Just as important, many people are fighting to protect pollinators in their communities—and you can, too! Check out these ways to help protect the bees and other pollinators.

GROW A GARDEN

Many pollinators need plants to survive. Planting a garden offers them more places to eat and rest!

PLANT LOCAL PLANTS

Have an adult help you research which plants and flowers are native to the area you live in. These plants can help your local pollinators thrive and also make the local ecosystem stronger.

PROVIDE WATER

Pollinators get thirsty! If you provide small sources of water (like a birdbath or something similar), pollinators can stop by for a sip.

MAKE A BEE HOTEL

Open a bee "hotel" in your backyard! Bee hotels are safe spots for solitary bees to make their nests. Turn to the next page to try making your own.

BUILD A BEE HOTEL

Bees help plants survive by moving pollen from one flower to another. Mason bees are important pollinators for fruit orchards. And you can help them by building a bee hotel, which is a safe place for them to lay their eggs. Don't worry, mason bees are not aggressive and generally don't sting unless provoked.

You Need

- Quart-size cardboard milk carton
- Scissors
- Duct tape
- Ruler
- About 75 paper straws
- Extra-long zip ties
- Cardboard box

1. Cut off the top of the milk carton. Thoroughly wash the carton and let it dry. Cover it with duct tape.

2. Cut the paper straws so they are six and a half inches long. Place them inside the bee hotel until it's snugly filled with straws.

3. In early spring, place your bee hotel outside. Look for a good spot that is near a flower garden and is at least three feet off the ground. It should get sunlight but be protected from wind and rain. A good location would be in the crook of some strong tree branches.

4. Point the opening of the hotel toward the morning sun and tilt it slightly down, so rain won't get inside. The eggs won't survive if the bee hotel swings in the wind, so tie it securely in place with zip ties.

Tip

Don't bother the bees. Mason bees rarely sting, but they may become aggressive if you disturb them. Mason bees need mud for the tubes, so keep a small pile of damp soil close to the bee hotel. If there are hungry birds in your garden, protect the bee eggs by wrapping some wire netting around the front of the bee hotel.

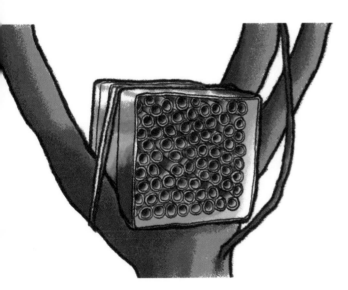

5. Take notes in an observation journal about any activity you see around your bee hotel. You may see a mason bee flying in and out, carrying mud or pollen into the tubes. After a mason bee has laid her eggs in a tube, she will plug up the entrance with mud.

6. In late June, take down the bee hotel very gently and put it inside a cardboard box in an unheated garage or shed. Inside the tubes, the eggs will hatch and the larvae will grow into adults.

7. When winter is almost over, put the bee hotel back outside, facing the sun. Over the next few weeks, the new bees will chew open the mud doors of their tubes and fly out to help pollinate the flowers. ■

How Do We Reduce Food Waste?

SOMETIMES, FOOD THAT ISN'T eaten can go bad and is thrown out. Other times, a person takes just a little too much on their plate and throws out what they can't eat. This food that isn't eaten or used is called *food waste*.

Small instances of food waste happen here and there, but it can add up over time. Places that deal with huge amounts of food like shipping companies, farms, restaurants, and supermarkets can also create a lot of food waste. Luckily, people around the world are working on ways to reduce this food waste. They're making sure that not only does food get used but that all people have enough to eat.

With help from technology and dedicated experts, global leaders and companies are cutting back on food waste by introducing new bills and tracking how food is used. But there are also things people can do right at home! Try these tips to help reduce food waste:

Using Scraps: Did you know that you can grow a whole new potato from the scraps of an old one? Or that you can bake mushy bananas into banana bread? Have an adult help you research ways to use those food odds and ends.

Smaller portions: It's better to go back for seconds—or thirds—than to take too much food and have to toss it. Try starting with smaller portions and getting more as you need it.

Write to your local leaders: Have an adult help you write a letter to a local government leader to ask them to help put a stop to food waste. Do some research on how other areas around the world are reducing food waste. If you think that any of those ideas could work for your community, include those ideas in the letter.

Composting: Composting is a way to help manage food waste. It's the process of turning food scraps back into soil that can be used to feed more plants. Have an adult help you try composting at home or see if a local garden composts.

COMPOSTING IN ACTION

Observe the process of composting with this activity.

You Need

- 2-liter plastic bottle
- Scissors
- Soil
- Old newspapers
- Food scraps (fruit and vegetables, teabags, coffee grounds, etc.)
- Dry leaves and grass clippings
- Spray bottle of water
- Duct tape
- Coffee can lid or plate

1. With help from an adult, cut the top third off the plastic bottle and poke small holes in the bottom and sides of the bottle.

2. Add a layer of soil to the bottom of the bottle. Then add a layer of newspaper. Next, add a layer of food scraps. Finally, add a layer of dead leaves and grass clippings. Spray with water.

3. Repeat step 2 until the bottle is filled. Do not pack the contents down as you add layers.

4. Place the top back on the bottle. Use duct tape to tape it closed.

5. Place the coffee can lid or plate under the bottle. Shake the bottle to mix the ingredients every few days. In two to three months, you will have beautiful soil! ■

Tip

There are lots of activities in this book that use food as an ingredient. Brainstorm ways that you can reuse or recycle some of the food materials in your experiments.

More Ideas

This activity lets you see composting in action. But it won't let you compost much of the plant waste you produce. If you'd like to compost on a larger scale, work with an adult to research a composting plan that works for your family.

How Do Wind and Water Create Power?

FROM OUR LIGHTS TO OUR CARS to the factories around us, much of the world today is powered by electric energy. But electricity has to come from somewhere. To produce electricity, many people and companies use *turbines*. A turbine is a rotating machine that uses blades to capture movement energy and turn it into electricity.

The most common fuels that people across the world use to get electricity from turbines are gas and coal. In this process, gas and coal are burned to boil water. The steam from this boiling water then turns the turbine's blades, creating movement, which is turned into electricity.

Unfortunately, these two fuels create tons of pollution, which harms the living things on our planet. Luckily, we can create electricity from other sources, too—including some that create much less pollution.

Wind and water are both clean sources of energy. Unlike gas or coal, which need to be burned to create electric energy, wind and water just need to move!

Electric energy created from water is known as *hydroelectricity*. Hydroelectric plants create electricity by harnessing the energy of moving water, such as in a river or the ocean. As the water moves, it flows through a turning wheel called a water turbine. A machine called a *generator* then turns the movement energy from the turbine into electricity.

Wind energy works in a similar way. In this case, wind turns the large blades of a tall type of turbine called a wind turbine—acting sort of like a giant windmill. As wind causes the turbine to spin, it powers an attached generator, creating electricity. With more and more of this clean energy, we can create less and less pollution.

BUILD A PINWHEEL

Make this colorful pinwheel to see how the blades of a wind turbine move.

You Need

- Colorful, heavy paper
- Scissors
- Ruler
- Sharpened pencil
- Straight pin with ball top
- Small bead
- Unsharpened pencil with eraser

1. Cut a piece of paper into a six-by-six-inch square.

2. Use the pencil and ruler to draw a light X from corner to corner on the paper, creating four smaller triangles. Make a dot in the center of the paper where the lines cross.

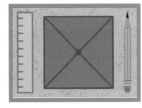

3. Cut on each diagonal line until you are about one inch from the center dot.

4. Beginning with the bottom right triangle, fold every other corner to the center dot. Do not crease the curved paper. Make

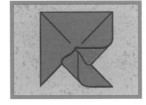

sure the corner tips overlap on top of the center dot.

5. Push the straight pin through the corner tips at the center of the pinwheel.

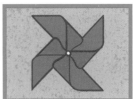

6. Slide a small bead onto the pin. Then push the end of the straight pin through the side of the eraser at the top of the pencil.

7. Hold your pinwheel and blow. Watch it spin!

How It Works:
The blades of a wind turbine change straight-line motion into circular or rotational motion. You can see how this works using your pinwheel. When you blow on a pinwheel, your breath flows in a straight line. When it hits the blades of the pinwheel at the right angle, the air turns the blades and the pinwheel spins in circles. ■

Tip
Glue two pieces of colorful paper together to make a two-sided pinwheel.

How Does Planting Trees Help the Planet?

TREES ARE INCREDIBLE—THEY DO so much for the planet and provide shelter for so many animals of all different shapes and sizes. But many trees are being cut down. This is called *deforestation*, or the large-scale removal of trees to make way for farms, cattle-grazing, cities, golf courses, and many other human activities. Sometimes the trees themselves are used for their wood. To fight against deforestation, people all over the world have come together to plant more trees and help regrow our forests.

So how, exactly, do trees make our planet a better place to live? Just like you need the gas oxygen to survive, trees need a gas called *carbon dioxide*. Carbon dioxide is part of what humans breathe out after they've taken oxygen into their bodies. It's also produced by many vehicles and factories as pollution. Too much carbon dioxide causes our planet to heat up and many living things to get sick. But because trees need carbon dioxide, they help clean our environment by taking the gas out of the air—and releasing oxygen in exchange!

Trees also help filter pollutants from our soils and water. And tree roots hold soil in place, preventing rain and wind from washing that soil away. On top of that, trees provide homes to countless living things, from animals that burrow in the dirt under their roots to birds that nest in their branches. So trees need us and we need them!

MAKE AN HERBARIUM

The more we discover about trees and plants, the more we can learn to appreciate them. An *herbarium* is a collection of leaves and flowers that can help people to identify plants.

You Need

- Leaves and flowers
- 2 book-size pieces of cardboard
- Old newspaper
- Heavy books
- Plain paper
- Glue
- Paintbrush
- Colored pencils and markers

1. Collect leaves and flowers. If they are wet, let them dry as much as possible.

2. Prepare the press: Lay a piece of newspaper on one of the pieces of cardboard.

3. Lay the leaves and flowers as flat as possible on the newspaper. Cover them with another piece of newspaper and then a piece of cardboard.

4. Stack heavy books on top of the pile and wait at least a week.

5. While you are waiting, with an adult's help, use online sources or books to learn more about your plants.

6. Check your leaves to see if they are completely dried out. Once they are dry, they are ready for the next step.

Tip
You only need one side of the plain paper to be blank, so recycle paper by using a piece that has something written on the other side!

7. Use the paintbrush to spread a thin layer of glue on a piece of paper.

8. Carefully move the dried leaves and flowers to the paper and press gently to make them stick.

9. Use the colored pencils and markers to label your herbarium. When you're done, recycle the paper! Make sure to remove the leaves and flowers first before recycling. ■

Tip
DO watch for poison ivy, so you don't accidentally pick some. DON'T take someone's flowers without their permission!

How Does Recycling Work?

YOU MAY HAVE HEARD THE phrase "reduce, reuse, and recycle." The first two are pretty straight-forward: Try to use and buy fewer things, and then use the things you do have as many times as you can before getting more. But recycling is a bit more complex.

Recycling is the act of breaking down waste materials and turning them into new things. This cuts down on the amount of trash sent to landfills. Recycled waste—like old tires, some plastics, metal, paper, and more—can be turned into brand-new objects such as clothes, containers, machine parts, and even roads.

The first step in recycling is to gather the waste. People at home place their recycling into special bins that are collected by workers. Next, workers and machines help separate all the materials by category (such as paper, plastic, metal, and more). These items are then cleaned.

A DIFFERENT WATER CYCLE

Solids aren't the only things that get recycled—water does, too! And not just in the natural water cycle. Scientists have found ways to treat dirty water—even the water flushed in people's toilets. They separate out the wastes and kill any germs. Then, the cleaned-up water can be used again.

After that—*smash!*—the different items are smushed together into large, condensed blocks of material. These blocks of plastic, paper, rubber, and more are then sent to different companies that use them to build and create new things.

Sometimes, items that can't be recycled turn up at recycling plants. These have to be sent back to land-fills, which is why it is important to pay close attention to what you are recycling. But as technology improves, scientists are finding innovative ways to recycle more and more things, and to make a fantastic future from recycled goods.

Cube of Materials
Ready for Recycling

REPURPOSE OLD THINGS INTO NEW STUFF

Learn how to reuse things that might normally have made their way into the trash.

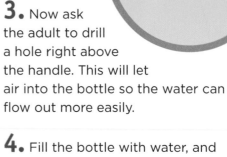

FROM A PLASTIC BOTTLE TO A WATERING CAN

You Need

- Empty laundry detergent bottle and lid, both clean
- Permanent marker
- Electric drill and ⅛- or ¹⁄₁₆-inch drill bit

1. Use the marker to make dots for about 10 holes in the lid. Space them so they are about one-half inch apart.

2. Screw the lid on to the bottle. Ask an adult for help using the drill to make a hole at each dot.

3. Now ask the adult to drill a hole right above the handle. This will let air into the bottle so the water can flow out more easily.

4. Fill the bottle with water, and then screw on the lid again. When your plants (like the onion garden from pages 262–263) need a drink, just tip the bottle and sprinkle the water over them!

**MAKE A PINHOLE CAMERA
OUT OF A USED BOX**

You Need

- Empty cardboard cereal box or oatmeal container
- Pencil
- Wax paper
- Tape or rubber band
- Blanket

1. Using a pencil, punch a hole in the center of the bottom of the box.

2. Place a piece of wax paper over the open end of the box and secure it with tape or a rubber band.

3. Sit in a dim room that has a bright object in it, such as a lamp. Put a blanket over your head and the camera.

4. Hold the camera at arm's length, with the wax paper toward you and the punched-out hole sticking out from under the blanket. Point the camera at the bright object. On the surface of the wax paper you will see a picture of the bright object—backward and upside down.

How It Works:
Pinhole cameras work because light travels in a straight line. Instead of a lens, the pinhole guides the light so that an upside-down image forms on the inside of the box. ■

How Can We Clean Plastic from Our Seas?

EVERY YEAR, MORE THAN EIGHT million tons of plastic end up in our ocean. This hurts the animals that live in the ocean and the ocean environment itself. Animals can get caught in the plastic or eat it and get sick if they mistake it for food. Plastic also takes a very long time to break down, meaning it remains in the ocean for many, many years.

Many people around the world are working to remove some of the plastic in the ocean. Some of these pieces of plastic are large. They can sometimes be removed using large nets that are safe for sea life but scoop up floating pieces of plastic. Other floating devices can snatch plastic as it drifts by.

Some plastic is trickier. Although plastic takes a very long time to completely break down, it still breaks down into smaller particles, called *microplastics*. These microplastics cannot simply be scooped from the ocean. That's why scientists and engineers are inventing new ways to tackle this pollution. Some scientists are studying bacteria that might be able to eat the microplastic. Others are searching for natural ways to filter out microplastics. And still other people are attempting to use magnetic coils that will break down the microplastics into harmless substances.

One of the most important parts of the fight against plastic is to prevent more plastics from entering the ocean. Some engineers and activists have created capture systems that collect plastic from rivers before it can enter the ocean. Because most rivers and streams drain into the ocean, focusing on these areas can be one of the best ways to cut down on plastics entering the seas.

However, the best way to prevent plastic from reaching the ocean is to cut down on the creation and use of plastic itself. Some leaders and activists are introducing laws to help ban single-use plastics (like plastic straws). Scientists are also introducing alternative materials—some of these are organic materials like bamboo, and others are man-made materials designed to break down after use.

Whatever method we use, it is important to keep up the fight against plastics in our oceans. Everyone can take part—including you!

Some of the activities in this book require the use of plastic materials. Instead of throwing them away after you're done, how can you reuse or recycle them?

DESIGN AN OCEAN CLEANING MACHINE

Earth's oceans can become polluted with litter, oil, and other waste. Design and make something to help remove waste from water.

You Need

- Large plastic bin
- Warm water
- Vegetable oil
- Cocoa powder
- Scissors
- Newspaper
- Coffee grounds
- Biodegradable coffee filters
- Sponge
- Comb
- Biodegradable dish soap

1. Fill the bin about three-fourths full with warm water. Mix a spoonful of cocoa powder into a few spoonfuls of vegetable oil. Drizzle the brown oil on the top of the water in the tub.

2. Use the scissors to cut a piece of newspaper into smaller pieces and sprinkle them into the water. This represents the plastic that can end up in waterways.

3. Add a couple spoonfuls of coffee grounds to the water.

4. Think about how you might be able to use the coffee filters, sponge, comb, and dish soap to clean the dirty water.

5. Use the materials to test your ideas. What works to make the water cleaner? ■

More Ideas

Use a paper and pencil to draw a machine that might be used to clean the real ocean based on what you learned in this experiment.

RESOURCES

Websites

For science activities and experiments:
https://www.sciencefun.org/kidszone/experiments/ for lots of science experiments

https://www.sciencebuddies.org for more science projects you can do

https://sciencebob.com for even more fun experiments you can do on your own

For information about taking care of the planet:
http://kids.nceas.ucsb.edu/index.html to learn about ecology, data science, biomes, and marine mammals

https://www.epa.gov/recycle/reduce-reuse-recycle-resources-students-and-educators for information about recycling

https://kids.nationalgeographic.com/nature/save-the-earth to learn about different ways you can help save Earth

https://www.audubon.org/news/how-kids-can-make-difference-birds-earth-day to learn how you can help care for birds

https://www.treehugger.com/meet-kids-who-are-changing-world-4868568 to meet 20 kids who are changing the world

For information about technology:
https://www.sciencemuseum.org.uk/objects-and-stories/everyday-technology for the stories behind everyday technologies

https://www.sciencekids.co.nz/sciencefacts/technology.html for information about all kinds of technology

https://www.lifehack.org/articles/technology/25-fun-apps-and-websites-teach-kids-about-technology.html for a list of apps and websites that will teach you about technology

For information about the human body:
https://kidshealth.org for information about kids' health

https://www.nationalgeographic.org/media/organization-and-structure-human-body/ to learn how the human body is organized

https://www.timeforkids.com/g56/topics/the-human-body/ for lots of articles about kids and their bodies

https://kids.niehs.nih.gov/index.htm for fun and educational materials about health, science, and the environment we live in today

For information about dinosaurs:
https://www.amnh.org/dinosaurs for tons of information from the American Museum of Natural History in New York

https://www.nhm.ac.uk/discover/dinosaurs.html for information from the Natural History Museum in London, England

https://kids.nationalgeographic.com/animals/prehistoric/ to explore the latest facts on dinosaurs with National Geographic Kids

For information about weather and climate:
https://climatekids.nasa.gov/menu/weather-and-climate/ for information about weather

https://www.weatherwizkids.com for information about weather, natural disasters, and experiments you can do

https://climatekids.nasa.gov for information and activities from NASA about climate change

https://www.weather.gov/owlie/science_kt for links, labs, and activities about weather from the National Weather Service

For information about the ocean:
https://oceanservice.noaa.gov/kids/ to discover all about the ocean and the changing world

https://ocean.si.edu for quick links about the ocean and ocean animals from the Smithsonian Institution

https://kids.earth.org/life-in-the-water/facts-about-ocean-plastic-pollution-for-kids/ to learn about ocean plastic

For information about outer space:
http://smithsonianeducation.org/supernova/supernova2.html to take an interactive tour through a supernova

https://mo-www.cfa.harvard.edu/MicroObservatory/ to explore the universe with telescopes you control over the internet

https://www.nasa.gov/stem for NASA STEM activities you can do at home

For information about food:
https://www.myplate.gov/life-stages/kids for activities and games that teach you about a healthy diet

https://ssec.si.edu/pick-your-plate to play a game about nutrition around the world

https://www.girlshealth.gov/nutrition/index.html for nutrition information just for girls

https://foodhero.org/kids for videos, activities, and kid-approved healthy recipes for all kinds of foods

Science Lab Tips

Follow these safety rules when you're doing science experiments:

• **Ask an adult to help.** Never touch any chemicals or lab equipment without permission.

• **Pick a safe place to do experiments.** You need an area with good ventilation and easy access to water. It should be high enough that younger children and pets can't reach it. The kitchen table might be a good option.

• **Act responsibly.** To avoid accidents, never run or mess around in a science lab.

• **Follow directions.** Mixing the wrong ingredients or the wrong amounts of ingredients can be dangerous.

• **Read labels.** Make sure you are using the right ingredients.

• **Keep your work area clean.** Wash your hands and your supplies before and after doing experiments. If you accidentally spill something, clean it up immediately.

• **Keep food and drinks out of the lab area.** It's too easy to contaminate your food or mix up stuff you want to eat with ingredients from your experiments.

• **Protect your eyes.** Accidents happen. Spills and splashes can get in your eyes. Always wear approved eye protection when doing experiments.

• **Dress like a scientist.** Always wear long pants and roll up loose sleeves. Wear an apron or lab coat to protect your clothes from stains or spills.

• **Protect your feet.** Always wear closed-toe shoes. Never do experiments in your bare feet.

• **Keep long hair tied back.** Long hair can dangle into or get caught in things.

• **Eliminate distractions.** Put away your phone and other devices that can interfere with your concentration.

• **Ask questions.** If you're not sure what to do, ask a friend or an adult for help. Or, take a break and search online to find the answer yourself.

• **Don't panic.** If you have an emergency, stay calm and immediately ask an adult for help.

Kitchen Tips

Follow these safety rules when you're cooking or baking:

• **Ask an adult to help.** It's important to have an experienced adult with you to help with anything hot or sharp, or to run appliances.

• **Wash your hands often.** Always wash them well with soap and water for at least 10 seconds before touching food. After you touch raw meat, poultry, fish, or egg products, immediately wash your hands.

• **Keep surfaces clean.** Wash your countertops or other surfaces thoroughly with warm water and soap both before and after using them.

• **Wash fruits and vegetables before cutting or eating them.** Even if a package label says it's organic, fresh, or just-picked, it's always best to give produce a good wash.

• **Wear oven mitts if you have permission to use the stove or oven.** Pots and pot handles on the stovetop can be burning hot. The same is true for pans in the oven and, sometimes, the microwave.

• **Turn pot or pan handles toward the back of the stove when you aren't holding them.** Someone walking by the stove could accidentally knock into the handle and cause the pan or hot food to fall.

• **Only use microwave-safe cookware in the microwave oven.** That means no metal, aluminum, or certain plastics should ever be in the microwave. They can melt or cause a fire.

• **If you're allowed to use a knife, follow these rules:** Never cut toward yourself, don't touch the sharp edge of the blade with your finger, and keep the hand not holding the knife away from the blade.

Other helpful hints:

• **How to measure dry ingredients:** Using the measuring tool (cup, teaspoon, tablespoon, etc.), scoop out the dry ingredient from its package. Then use a butter knife or other straight edge to level it off over the package it came from. Or, spoon dry ingredients into your measuring tool, and then level it off.

• **How to measure wet ingredients:** Use a clear measuring cup with a pour spout. Set the cup on a flat surface and pour liquid ingredients into it. Bend down to the surface level and look at the cup straight on to see if it's at the measurement you want.

Index

Z

Credits

WRITERS

Ana Appel (22); Andrew Brisman (300); Sarah Chapman (270, 324); Lisa Glover (32, 176); Amy S. Johnson (48); Laurie Kane (300); Carmen Morais (45, 314); Libby Romero and Jennifer Szymanski (all other activities); Paige Towler (all science explanations)

ILLUSTRATORS

Sebastian Abboud (6, 64, 186, 244); Lynn Adams (244); Paula Becker (292); Tim Budgen (187); Scott Burroughs (187, 192-193, 214-215, 229, 238, 241, 247, 274-275, 280-281, 292-293, 310-311); Jenny Campbell (45); Hayelin Choi (11, 12-13, 21, 26-27, 39, 58-59, 70-71, 85, 100-101, 126, 127, 136, 159, 169, 177, 182, 196, 219, 222-223, 266-267, 288-289, 319, 325); David Coulson (15, 99, 198, 259, 268, 318); Mike Dammer (280); Linda Davick (124); Jack Desrocher (36, 87, 97); T.M. Detwiler (7, 15, 25, 50, 51, 54-55, 88-89, 108-109, 125, 144-145, 166-167, 180-181, 200-201, 232-233, 240, 246-, 258-259, 296-297); Dougal Dixon (107, 119); Avram Dumitrescu (19, 30, 32-33, 42-43, 76-77, 99, 132-133, 137, 160, 172-173, 188-189, 208-209, 221, 262-263, 304-305, 314-315); Joey Ellis (124); Travis Foster (308); Rocky Fuller (79, 124); Mernie Gallagher-Cole (156); David Helton (6, 36); Jannie Ho (141); Tom Jay (cover, intro page, 4-5, 6, 34-35, 62-63, 94-95, 122-123, 148, 154-155, 184-185, 186, 210-211, 212, 242-243, 276-277, 278, 306-307, 308, 328, 334-342); Dave Joly (28); Kelly Kennedy (262, 273, 309, 310, 158); Dave Klug (72); Vicky Lommatzsch (22-23, 44, 93, 176, 270-271, 300-301, 324); Mike Lowery (36); Gareth Lucas (208); Mike Moran (115, 164, 168); Jim Paillot (106); Patrick M. Pelz (30-31); Janet Robertson (244); Carmen Saldana (312); Rico Schacherl (87); Dan Sipple (9, 16-17, 37, 41, 56, 67, 69, 82, 104-105, 120-121, 130, 131, 135, 152-153, 162-163, 183, 204-205, 218, 226-227, 236-237, 250-251, 284-285, 327); Scott Soeder (85); Robert Squier (98, 114, 118); Jason Tharp (10); Beegee Tolpa (48-49); Dave Whamond (308); Pete Whitehead (206); Kevin Zimmer (234)

PHOTOS

Key: GI=Getty Images, SS=Shutterstock, GCAI= Guy Cali Associates, Inc. 7: Liliboas/GI (pizza); 8: _LeS_/GI (chocolate bar); 8-9: Tim UR (top); 10: Prostock-Studio/GI (top); 12: ADELART/GI (beads); 14: NASA/Aubrey Gemignani; 18: klosfoto/GI; 20: rakim-/GI (batteries), pookpiik/GI (drone); 24: Lefteris_/GI; 26: FineArtCraig/GI (pennies); 28: NickyLloyd/GI (girl); 29: GCAI (tape), MarkSwallow/GI (watering can); 36: Elena

Mitrokhina/GI (comb); 37: Graham Montanari/GI (curls); 38 akvafoto/GI (bubbles), Anastasiia_M / GI (shampoo), tanuha2001/GI (olive oil), airdone / GI (hair); 40: parinyabinsuk/GI; 41: karandaev/GI (grass); 46: D. Hurst/Alamy; 47: Martin Dimitrov/GI; 49: prairie_eye/GI (scoop); 50: AJ_Watt/GI (boy); 52: TheCrimsonMonkey/GI (burger), D. Hurst/Alamy (fork); 53: Vasko/GI (pizza), vmenshov/GI (orange), malerapaso /GI (chili), Floortje/GI (avocado); 54: sangfoto/GI (crackers); 57: Nina Shannon/GI(top), Jupiterimages/GI (center), Prostock-Studio/GI (bottom); 58: ryasick/GI (balloons); 60: indianeye/GI; 61: Floortje/GI; 64: Rosinka/GI (cat), neyro2008/GI (crab, hedgehog), 65: GlobalP/GI; 66: PetlinDmitry/GI; 67: Dieter Spears; 68: cyoginan/GI; 70: Лилия Альбертовна Галеева/GI; 72: SikorskiFotografie/SS (dog photo); 73: Suzannah Skelton/GI (pickles), Tim UR /GI (onion), YinYang/GI (cookies); 74: GlobalP/GI; 75: Mckyartstudio/GI; 78: Coatesy/GI; 79: malerapaso/GI (bike); 80-81: slowmotiongli/GI; 81: Tonkovic/GI; 84 Creative Nature/GI; 86: Superstock; 87: Gerald and Buff Corsi/Focus on Nature/GI (blowhole), Tania Bondar/GI (music); 90: Liliboas/GI; 91: Sam Stukel/USFWS; 92 Jim Hudgins/USFWS; 96 Iryna Bodnaruk (triceratops), Hachio Nora/G (tree, feathered dino), setory/GI (pasta); 97 LeventKonuk/GI (skeleton), 97 hsvrs/GI (trilobite); 100: Iurii Garmash/GI (leaves); 102-103 estt/GI; 103 Kenneth Canning/GI (hummingbird); 104: fcafotodigital/GI; 106: jarino47/GI (eggs); 107: meen_na/GI (oviraptor); 110: suriyasilsaksom/GI; 111: orla/GI; 112: YvanDube/GI; 113: NiseriN/GI; 116: sb-borg/GI (binoculars), N. Lewis/NPS (bird); 117: ArtMassa/GI; 119 CoreyFord/GI (bottom); 124: Cheremuha/GI (tracks), Mellok/GI (shell), 128: Lukas Bischoff/GI; 129: Frank Ramspott/GI; 134-135: SalvoV/GI; 138-139: Marina Lohrbach/GI; 139: John Plant/Alamy (rafflesia); 140: Tetiana Rostopira/GI (cinnamon), nectarine/GI (petals); 142: habrda/GI (top), Olga Potylitsyna/GI; 143: Cerise HUA/GI (branches), dmackieboy /GI (brick), Viorika /GI (sky), SimplyCreative-Photography/GI (roof), aleksandarvelasevic/GI (background); 146-147: Lukas Bischoff/GI; 147: tzooka/GI (fox); 148-149: Judit Hoffmann/GI (background); 149: Marek Uliasz/GI (top left), 3quarks/GI (top right), Aviator70/GI (center left), AlexmarPhoto/GI (center right), Mark Aventino/GI (bottom); 150: FrankvandenBergh/GI; 151 tbralnina/GI (leaves), SeppFriedhuber/GI (fox); 156: rambo182/GI (snowflake), AnnaFrajtova/GI (clouds); 159: ValentynVolkov/GI (ice); 161: mdesigner125/GI; 165: Irina Meshcheryakova/GI; 170: BrianAJackson/GI; 171: NASA/JPL-Caltech/UA; 174: Noppharat05081977/GI; 175: JenDeVos/ GI (birds), OgnjenO/GI (branches), tchara/GI (hail); 178: Francis Lavigne-Theriault/GI; 179: 3DSculptor/GI; 180-181: OlgaLebedeva/GI (glitter); 182: urbancow/GI (background); 186: gmm2000/GI (notebook), neyro2008/GI (octopus); 187: Damocean/GI (background), 190: akiyo/GI; 191: StevenDillon/GI; 194-195: Andrea Zanchi/GI; 195: Georgette Douwma/GI (fish); 197 hkuchera/GI (top), kcline/GI (bottom); 199: Eloi_Omella/GI; 201: Oxford Scientific/GI; 202: bullantmultimedia/GI; 202-203: Oleandra9/GI (background); 203: Kamila Kozioł/GI; 204: mazzzur/GI; 205: Palle Christensen/GI; 206: Gabriele Grassl/GI (penguins); 207: Ondrej Prosicky/GI; 213: Onkamon Buasorn/GI; 216: Cherelliss/GI; 217: dem10/GI; 220: SusanneSchulz/GI; 221: Lost_in_the_Midwest/SS (glasses); 222: deepblue4you (cream cheese); 223: chorboon_photo/GI (crackers), photomaru/GI (cucumber); 224: 3quarks/GI; 225: NASA/JPL/MSSS; 226: walterbilotta/GI (penne), jenifoto/GI (lasagna); 227: Nahhan/GI (wheel pasta), NASA/JPL-Caltech (blueprint); 228: NASA/ESA/Hubble; 231: NASA/JPL-Caltech; 232: Eivaisla/GI (foil); 233: MaskaRad/G (fruit); 235: bjdlzx/GI; 237: Claudio Caridi/GI (meteorite), unalozmen/GI (chocolate); 239: Tatyanash/GI; 240: AlasdairJames/GI (rice); 244: setory/GI (sandwich); 245: GCAI; 246: GCAI (raisins); 248: Inna Tarasenko/GI (seeds), Mariusz-Blach/GI (pumpkin); 249: StudioBarcelona/GI; 250-252: LENA/GI (slime); 252-253: solidcolours/GI (top); 253: valentinarr/GI (strawberry), Stockbyte/GI (pumpkin), photomaru/GI (olives), Dimitris66/GI (tomato), Boonchuay1970/GI (chilis); 254: Adam Smigielski/GI; 255: Larry_Herfindal/GI (bananas), jskiba/GI (bag); 256-257: fcafotodigital/GI; 257 bildobjektiv (inset); 260-261: SageElyse/GI; 261: Tim UR/GI (inset); 264: lucielang/GI; 265: sasapanchenko/GI (apples), gemenacom /GI (banana); 266: pepmiba/GI (apples); 269: Bhubatet/GI; 270: arcimages/GI (candy); 272: Yasonya/GI (mint), ImagePixel/GI (gum): Sideways Design/GI (candy cane); 275: MariaTkach/GI (candy); 278: barbulat/GI (shadow), Frank Ramspott/GI (blocks); 279: Anton Podoshvin/GI; 282: Martin Keiler/GI; 283: Lionbig/GI; 286-287: skodonnell/GI; 288: Science Photo Library/Superstock (crayons); 291: gbh007/GI; 294: aga7ta/GI; 295: JMichl/GI; 296-297: alenaohneva/GI (bubbles); 298: StanRohrer/GI; 299: FreedomMaster/GI (all); 302-303: coffeekai/GI; 313: a8096b40_190/GI; 314: HHelene/GI (bee); 316: GaryAlvis/GI; 317: KariHoglund/GI; 320: Maksym Bondarchuk/SS; 321: photka/GI; 322: Laboko/GI (top), ranplett/GI (bottom); 323: Dony/GI; 326: AndreyPopov/GI; 327: GCAI

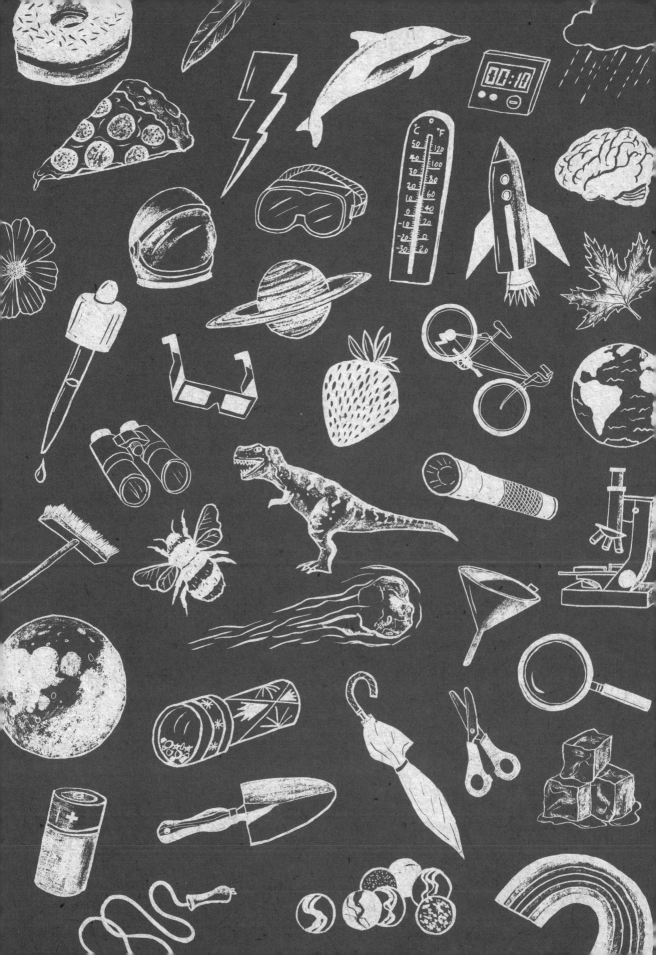